# Evangelical and Evolving

## Following the gospel in a changing world

## Colin Craston

CANTERBURY
PRESS
Norwich

© Colin Craston 2006

First published in 2006 by the Canterbury Press Norwich
(a publishing imprint of Hymns Ancient & Modern Limited,
a registered charity)
9–17 St Alban's Place, London
N1 0NX

www.scm-canterburypress.co.uk

British Library Cataloguing in Publication data

A catalogue record for this book is available
from the British Library

ISBN 1-85311-751-X/978-1-85311-751-0

Typeset by Regent Typesetting, London
Printed and bound by
Bookmarque Ltd, Croydon, Surrey

# Contents

To my wife and colleague, Brenda

# Foreword

In the journey of life we are subjected to many influences. These factors can either change our outlook or cement us further in our personal convictions. They can also provide us with opportunities to develop our thinking, enlarge our vision and deepen our understanding, while leaving our earlier convictions as some sort of starting-point rather than a destination.

In the Christian journey of life the imagery of a pilgrimage takes us close to the real meaning of the call of the incarnate Christ. That journey will move us through experiences in which we learn as much about ourselves as about '*the faith once delivered*'. The one certainty which we may or may not recognize is that we never stand still.

Colin Craston has been, is and undoubtedly will remain a convinced evangelical on that journey. But in this book with great integrity and attractive honesty he writes about changing attitudes, developing understanding and widening horizons. He chooses to describe those personal experiences as a process of evolving and in so doing shares landmarks in his journey which have also shaped the recent history of the Church of England and the wider Anglican Communion.

Colin has been uniquely placed to wed those milestones of Anglican life with personal attitudes. A lifetime of parochial ministry, membership of the General Synod of the Church of

England, membership of the Crown Appointments Commission, Chairmanship of the Anglican Consultative Council and involvement in many aspects of church life were to follow an upbringing in the evangelical tradition. War service gave him insights into the human condition which undoubtedly influenced the gifts he brought to ordination but it was his pilgrimage within the active ministry of the Church of God which has compelled him to stand back now and review what has led him to his present analysis of the role of an evangelical.

In this book he takes us along a personal story. He does not presume to regard that story as typical of the experiences of other evangelicals but his concluding words compel the reader to ponder important ingredients in understanding his claims to have moved forward on the road of Christian understanding:

> A tradition, while committed to its basic foundation truths, must evolve if it is to remain alive and responsive to new truth.

I find a refreshing honesty and openness in these pages. In an age in which Christianity has faced continous questioning about relevance and relationship to other faiths and Anglicanism has become involved in tensions and divisions which have shaken the Communion to its foundations, Colin Craston asks questions which go far beyond his personal pilgrimage.

Whatever our traditional outlook may be I believe this book has the ring of truth which must compel the reader to re-examine attitudes and question assumptions and in so doing enrich his or her own pilgrimage.

+Robert Armagh
*February 2006*

# Introduction

The year 2003 marked a significant phase in the development of the evangelical tradition in the Church of England, with reverberation in other parts of the Anglican Communion. The different strands of that tradition became more clearly identified in reaction to several events. The appointment of Dr Rowan Williams as Archbishop of Canterbury, the move to appoint a gay but celibate canon as Bishop of Reading, the appointment of a gay canon, divorced from his wife and living with another man, as Bishop of New Hampshire with the backing of a majority in the General Convention of the Episcopal Church of the United States of America (ECUSA) and its House of Bishops, the approval of same-sex 'marriages' in a Canadian diocese, and the fourth National Evangelical Anglican Congress (NEAC) at Blackpool, all happened within the space of a few months. The sexuality dimension in four of those five events is worthy of note. Not for the first time the Church found itself in dispute over sex. In the 25 years I served on General Synod the debates that caused most heat, but not always equivalent light, concerned marriage and divorce, cohabitation, homosexuality and women's ordination.

It is true that while the year 2003 focused so much on sexuality, evangelicals were rooting the problem more deeply in the authority and interpretation of Scripture. The charge against those of the liberal tradition was of elevating experience in the modern world above the Bible, of failing to acknowledge the Bible's supreme authority in discernment of God's will. While all evangelicals continued to hold to that position, there was no unanimity on how the crisis should be handled, nor on how the Scriptures should be interpreted and applied. The most intransigent line was taken by Reform (a network of conservative churches within the Church of England), begun earlier in opposition to the ordination of women, and Church Society ('strongly committed to the supreme and final authority of the Bible as God's Word Written'). These were strongly vocal in opposition to Dr Williams's appointment, allegedly because of his liberal attitude to homosexuality. In response to the proposed appointment of the Bishop of Reading another grouping emerged, Anglican Mainstream, presumably not entirely in accord with Reform. From NEAC another group, Fulcrum, was formed, committed to charitable debate with other traditions in Anglicanism. The reflections of these English reactions in the rest of the Communion focused on the extraordinary primates' meeting called by the Archbishop of Canterbury in October 2003 in response to the New Hampshire appointment. Fierce reaction from evangelical and other traditionalist primates from the two-thirds world was not surprising, although, again, little attention was given to the principles of biblical interpretation.

The year 2003 was not a unique manifestation of differences among evangelicals. However, attempts were then made to define more clearly the character of the groupings. An article in *Anvil*, the evangelical quarterly, by Canon Dr Graham Kings, Vicar of St Mary's, Islington, used the metaphor of watercourses. Canal, river and rapids were the descriptions given to conservative evangelicals, open evangelicals and charismatic evangelicals. 'The canal is direct and straight and its channel is blasted through obstacles: the river is indirect and meandering and moves around things in its pathway'.[1] Rapids he defined as characterized by vitality and energy.

In 2004 appeared the first of a five-volume history of the evangelical movement over the last three hundred years published by IVP. The first volume, *The Rise of Evangelicalism* by Mark A. Noll, one of the joint editors of the series, describes the age of Edwards, Whitefield and the Wesleys in an authoritative, thoroughly researched study.[2] While applauding the revitalization of Protestant Christianity in the English-speaking world, Noll frankly exposes the divisions within the leadership of the new movement and the barriers created. It is a revealing story of how human weakness, concerns and sensitivities are all mixed up with the Holy Spirit's working out God's purposes without us fully recognizing them.

Whatever the professed unity of evangelicals, and the variety of structures devised to achieve united action, their differences have certainly been evident for the past century. In 1922 the Church Missionary Society (CMS), since its conception firmly in the evangelical tradition, was riven by disagreement over what should be required of its missionaries. Commitment to an infallibilist and inerrancy view of Scripture, articulated by such as B. B. Warfield in America, was demanded by some in the Society. The split led to the founding of the Bible Churchmen's Missionary Society (BCMS). The basis of belief it adopted took the strongly conservative line. As a student at the college the Society founded, Tyndale Hall, formerly the Bible Missionary Theological College, I heard Dr Daniel Bartlett, a founding father of the Society, declare that if only the parent society had been willing to make an absolute commitment to 'the truth of all Christ's utterances' a split could have been avoided. From the 1920s, then, the tradition had liberal evangelical and conservative evangelical wings. While the former continued and had some representation in the leadership of the Church of England, the latter became a dwindling influence, small in numbers, isolated within established parishes and a few like-minded societies. A sense of paranoia prevailed. All this was while Anglo-Catholicism in the Church of England was at its most dominant stage.

After World War Two the first signs of recovery became evident. A fair proportion of ex-servicemen accepted for training for ordination were evangelically inclined. Confidence grew and in 1963 a successful Northern Evangelical Conference took place. It was organized by clergy from both sides of the Pennines. I am concentrating on that event because it is one I knew of first hand. I recall that on the committee it was resolved to keep the organizing of the event in our own hands rather than involve societies based in London – northern independence! The response to the conference was enthusiastic and in a plenary session there was a call from the floor not only for another similar event in 1965 but on a national basis. As a member of the committee I was asked to put the suggestion to Dr John Stott who was due to preach for me in Bolton later that year. He warmly supported the idea and together with representatives from the north, from Eclectics, a group of younger evangelicals, and evangelical societies the planning for NEAC 1 at Keele began. In the meantime, however, there were rumblings of secession from some clergy out of concern for developments in canon law revision then grinding its way though the Church Assembly. The fear was of declension from the Church's Protestant tradition. So in 1966 a conference entitled 'Facing the Future' was held at Swanwick with the aim of holding evangelicals in the Church of England. The paper I was asked to give was entitled 'The Limits of Compromise'.

Previous to these conferences there had been attempts to organize structures to enable united action. In 1950 the Church Association, strongly Protestant, and the National Church League, probably less so, came together to form the Church Society. And in 1960 the Church of England Evangelical Council was formed aiming to be representative of evangelical thought and action. It has had strong connections with evangelical unions in the dioceses.

The 1960s, and particularly the Anglican Evangelical Congress at Keele in 1967, arguably marked the highest degree of evangelical unity in the Church of England. Numbers were growing, greater influence was being exerted on national and diocesan structures, scholars of theological and biblical academic quality were making their mark. In 1959 Latimer House had been established to promote scholarly research and writing in the evangelical tradition. My own judgement is that it failed to fulfil the high expectations held at its beginning

A successor to Keele 1967 was evidently required, and took place as NEAC 2 at Nottingham in 1977. It was, as ten years before, a success, but from it emerged early signs of later division. One of the major themes was hermeneutics, well presented by Professor Tony Thiselton. To more conservative delegates this presentation seemed a dangerous move away from what they believed was the established position on the authority and interpretation of the Bible. Concern in these quarters grew, married to a determination to achieve increased influence in evangelical societies. A virtual take-over of Church Society came about. Its quarterly journal, *The Churchman*, came under a stricter editorial policy, with the result that evangelicals unhappy with that restriction established *Anvil* to represent the evangelical tradition as widely as possible. *Anvil* has certainly established itself as the major forum of evangelical thought. Less successful attempts on other societies were made. The Church Pastoral Aid Society, for instance, remained broadly based. One of the theological colleges, Oakhill, seemed to be most favoured by the conservatives. Then, after the ordination of women as priests, Reform got under way. Their influence on the Church of England Evangelical Council seemed to outsiders to be out of proportion to their support in the country generally, not least in the arrangements for NEAC 4 (2003) at Blackpool, particularly when at first the Archbishop of Canterbury was to be excluded but later given a diminished role. The *Church of England Newspaper* has continued to be a forum of evangelical thinking and activity.

This admittedly sketchy outline of where we have come from serves as a prelude to the theme of this book – the story of how one person evolved from a most rigid evangelical tradition to an open, perhaps very open, evangelical position. It is necessarily personal. Other open evangelicals will map a somewhat different route, agreeing or disagreeing with the response to the different issues. That is inevitable in the openness. No tight adherence to a detailed comprehensive statement and programme is acceptable. But it is not a case of 'anything goes'. We are totally committed to the cardinal doctrines of the faith: the Trinity, the person and work of Christ, his saving death and resurrection, the regenerating and sanctifying work of the Holy Spirit, the certain hope of Christ's parousia, the authority of Scripture. The Book of Common Prayer and the provisions of Common Worship are gladly accepted, and there is no real problem with the historic formularies. But what open evangelicals cannot do is claim to be absolutely and always right in their interpretation of Scripture, while others who differ are seriously and always wrong. They do not believe that evangelicalism is the only authentic expression of Anglicanism. They can learn from other traditions. Indeed, not this side of eternity will they infallibly know God's will. In short, what they believe is held with deep conviction, but in any respect they may be mistaken, for here we walk by faith, not sight, and see only through a glass darkly. There is continual need to recognize the partiality and inadequacy of all our concepts of God and his ways. Not even in heaven will we come to an end of discovery of his mystery and majesty. We do not desire to see a monochrome evangelical churchmanship across the Church of England or the whole Communion, as, for instance, the Diocese of Sydney, Australia, seems intent on creating.

I become increasingly convinced that temperament plays a greater part in the range of stances evangelicals adopt, and the same is true of other traditions, liberal and catholic. A sense of security arises for some from having convictions firmly formulated in a coherent whole. The removal of one brick from the arch, so to speak, could lead to the collapse of the whole. Or, to change the metaphor, one step on the slippery slope will lead to disaster. Loss of the familiar threatens security. One sees this in some folk in a congregation with changes in worship, new services instead of the old prayer book, new songs for old hymns.

Very many people, especially those with busy lives, yearn to know the truth in a simple, uncomplicated way. Attraction to the Roman Catholic Church meets this need for some laity. And indeed Cardinal Newman, disturbed by conflicting concepts in the Church of England, moved over to Rome to find an authority plainly demonstrated. Others are attracted to a fundamentalist expression of the faith based on a literalist approach to Scripture. Give it me straight and simple, is their concern.

The open stance, I believe, recognizes the need for inner security, sees that the slippery slope has its dangers. Abandon, or even feel doubtful about one point and it will be easier to move from others. But, ultimately, security can never really be in things, doctrinal statements, forms of worship or pattern of life, but in relationship. As everyone enters life needing to find security in relationship to mother and close family, and as life develops in loving relationships, so our only certain and lasting security is in relationship with our Saviour God. Secure in him changes can be faced, new truths enhanced, everything we hold tested and tried. The Bible story, it seems, bears this out. The Israelites redeemed from Egypt had to learn to follow God who went before them into unknown territory, however much tempted to return to the imagined security of Egypt.

There is a tendency in all ecclesiastical traditions towards intransigence on positions held dear. This is true, I believe, of evangelical, catholic and liberal traditions alike. We have got the truth, is the underlying conviction; others are defective in their understanding, or just plain wrong. It is believed that the honour of God's revealed will is at stake and it is up to us to defend it. What may not be recognized is a concern for one's feeling of security in the position held. But no one and no one tradition has the whole truth. The totality of God's ways is beyond our comprehension. No one has infallibility in interpretation of his revelation, although it is honourable to hold firmly but charitably to what one believes.

An illustration of the point I am making occurred for me in 1993. The Anglican Consultative Council (ACC), of which I was chairman at the time, was meeting in South Africa. Encouraged by some evangelicals in England, certain lay leaders of the Church of England in South Africa (CESA) strongly urged me to persuade the Archbishop of Canterbury, George Carey, to admit CESA into the Anglican Communion. Since the Colenso dispute in the late nineteenth century their church had been separated from the Church of the Province of South Africa (CPSA). I had to explain that the archbishop had no power of himself to admit them. Any church or province was admitted by decision of the primates and the ACC. So long as the two churches were unreconciled there could be no change. Efforts had been made to bring them closer together. In the mid-1980s Archbishop Robinson of Sydney, with the agreement of the primate of CPSA, and the support of the Archbishop of Canterbury, Robert Runcie, had consecrated a priest of his own diocese as bishop of CESA. It was a move towards the reconciliation of the two churches. Before long that bishop, Dudley Ford, resigned in frustration at the intransigence of CESA's members. Also in the 80s a consultation between some clergy from each church attempted in confidentiality ended when lay leaders in CESA found out. CESA believes itself to be absolutely loyal to the Anglican tradition but has been unwilling to be reconciled to CPSA, presumably because the latter has other traditions besides those that are undoubtedly evangelical.

I was born into and grew up before World War Two in a most strict and narrow evangelicalism. I am ever grateful for the faith, prayers and example of my parents. The Christian context, however, was firmly confined. The only 'real' Christians were evangelicals who had been converted in a recognizable pattern. The Bible was literally true in every respect. All 'worldliness' was forbidden – cinema, theatre, dancing, alcohol, transport on Sunday, smoking, raffles, even mention of sex. Evangelism was promoted almost wholly through campaigns and missions. Growth in holiness was heavily committed to the teaching of the annual Keswick (Bible) Convention. Prayer meetings and support of missionary work overseas featured strongly in the Christian community.

If I have moved somewhat from that way of life, adopted new positions, it is not because I resented that way at the time. It seemed to me as a teenager right and natural. Moving away at the age of 18 to four and a half years in the Navy began a process of reassessment, which continued through university and college and has gone on ever since. So, I move on to those areas of faith and practice in which reassessment has happened with me. I deal with them not in chronological order. They are the Bible, the Church, ministry, the sacraments, worship and liturgy, mission, eschatology, culture and the world, moral questions. I conclude with an attempt to justify my claim still to be an evangelical.

# I

# The Bible

In the world in which I grew up every verse, every line of the Bible was a direct word from God for the Christian, although one must admit that attention was generally restricted to selected passages – a tendency not unknown today. The Epistles, particularly of Paul, were the chief source of teaching, with use of the stories of the Gospels as illustrations. I suspect there was some unease with aspects of the teaching of Jesus on the kingdom of God. If, for instance, on Judgement Day we were to be judged on the basis of good works to the hungry and poor how did that fit in with being justified by grace through faith, not of works? Selectivity was very prevalent in respect of the Old Testament. The Schofield Reference Bible was our preferred version and its dipensationalist commentary shaped our understanding of the Bible's message. Scripture Union lectionaries with their notes were the basis of the obligatory daily 'quiet time' for the committed Christian. After demobilization, I began ordination training and became aware that other very different ways of looking at the Bible from the one I had grown up with existed in the Church. Although residing in Tyndale Hall, Bristol, I did not take the normal General Ordination Course, as after graduating at Bristol University I took a degree in theology as an external student of London University. For that there were no lectures in the Hall. However, from fellow students there

I realized their general attitude was that while it was necessary to swot up all 'the critical stuff' for examinations, after ordination it could be left behind. The BD course had anyway necessitated facing awkward questions concerning the Bible.

A curacy at St Nicholas, Durham, with John Wenham followed ordination. At that church there was provision for an annual lecture given by the vicar. One that had a deep effect on me was 'Total Inerrancy or Essential Infallibility?' The details are now dimly remembered, but it had the effect of convincing me that total inerrancy of the Scriptures as we now have them was not a view I could hold. But the entirely trustworthy presentation of God's saving purposes and his will for the redeemed community was what the Bible was given for. To know the way to heaven, to put it simply, the Scriptures were an infallible guide.

About this time I began to question one point of the Intervarsity Fellowship outlook. It was the attributing of inerrancy to the autographa, the original documents of Scripture. How could a dogmatic assertion concerning something to which we have no access be maintained? If in his saving purpose God had so controlled all the human authors to exclude every error he had not so controlled all the copying of the texts through several centuries. The only Bible we can know is a compilation of many texts with their variations. As someone has written recently, the text of Scripture is everywhere and nowhere, everywhere in a range of texts, and nowhere, as far as the originals are concerned. Many Christians in the apostolic age did not use the original documents of their Scriptures, the Old Testament, but a Greek version of the Hebrew in the Septuagint. It is worthy of note that 2 Timothy 3.16 describing all Scripture as 'God-breathed' is addressed to Timothy, for whom the Scriptures known since childhood were the Septuagint version, with its variations from the Hebrew texts. Today the vast majority of Christians do not have access to the extant manuscripts of the various texts, but rely on a number of versions in their own languages, some with considerable interpretation of the text built in. None of this adds up to any diminution of the claim that in Scripture we have an infallible word of God's saving purposes. It is not hard to suppose a motivation for the claims concerning the autographa. God is utterly trustworthy. If he wills to communicate with humanity his word must be without error, so the trustworthiness of God and the absolute trustworthiness of the text of Scripture are said to be intrinsically related. An interesting insight on this matter comes from NEAC 1 at Keele in 1967. Having been asked to chair the groups responsible for the doctrinal section of the congress report I suggested to the eight people associated with me in the preparation of the text that we should avoid use of the term 'infallibility' in the paragraphs on the Bible, on the grounds that adequate treatment of the concept would necessitate at least a substantial essay. These colleagues, all with theological expertise, fully agreed. When the draft statement was presented to sub-plenary and then plenary sessions the omission was not questioned.

In 1994 there appeared in the USA a book entitled *The Scandal of the Evangelical Mind*, by Mark A. Noll, himself an evangelical. His opening sentence reads: 'The scandal of the evangelical mind is that there is not much of an evangelical mind.' He acknowledges that appeal to the inerrancy of the autographa was strongly maintained by B. B. Warfield and A. A. Hodge at Princeton seminary in the late nineteenth century. But Noll himself says: 'when fundamentalists defended the Bible, they did so by arguing for the inerrancy of Scripture's original autographs, an idea that had been around for a long time but that had never assumed such a central role for any Christian movement.'[3]

If the Scriptures bring us the word of God, his self-disclosure for our salvation, they have an authority of unique status. The theologian who has had a major influence on my theological development is P. T. Forsyth (1848–1921), described by Emil Brunner and J. K. Mozeley as the greatest dogmatic theologian Great Britain has given to the Church in modern times. He writes in *The Principle of Authority* as follows.

> The Christian revelation is authoritative, or it is no Revelation . . . The principle of authority is ultimately the whole religious question. An authority of any practical kind draws its meaning and its right only from the soul's relation to its God. This is so not only for religion strictly so-called, nor for a Church, but for public life, social life, and the whole history and career of humanity.[4]

According to Forsyth, the establishment of this authority was the indispensable basis of true freedom, and the Christian faith alone can provide an authority whose very nature creates freedom.

Authority cannot be simply external or simply subjective.

> A real authority is indeed within our experience Forsyth maintains, but it is not the authority *of* experience; it is an authority *for* experience, an authority experienced . . . it is something given us. What is in us only recognises it. And the conscience which now recognises it has long been created by it.

We here think not just of that which ought to rule a person, but what in fact does rule a person. So, our final authority is not just God in the abstract, nor even the medium of the Scriptures, but a holy God coming to us through Jesus

Christ, redeeming and renewing through the cross, coming
to the soul, breaking it down in grace and restoring it in grace
– what Forsyth calls 'the evangelical experience'. We may
illustrate the truth in this way. Why believe a particular
aspect of Christian truth, say, the resurrection? I might
answer: because the Bible tells me so, or the Church teaches
it, or it commends itself to my reason. That prompts the
further question, Why believe the Bible? Or the Church? Or
trust the judgement of reason? Forsyth's answer would be:
because the word of God, subduing and renewing, has come
to me through Christ with self-authenticating power, convincing me that the word objectively revealed in history,
recorded in the Bible and proclaimed in the Church is true.
Authority, then, is always within a relationship of a personal
nature with God within, working with me and bringing me
into harmony with himself. It is direct, convincing, converting.

How then may we define more clearly the role of the
Scriptures? Forsyth starts from the word of God which is the
living Christ of the cross, God's personal act and presence.
That act and presence in history evokes from humanity a
witness in words, God himself evoking the verbal witness,
giving account of himself, interpreting his act and presence.
This is Forsyth's understanding of inspiration. Using the
illustration of the cross, he says it would not have been
sufficient for God merely to have acted: 'The deed without
the kerygma would have been dumb, and no Revelation.'
Many saw the cross to whom it meant nothing. He uses the
analogy of a tuning fork. 'God smote upon the world in
Christ's act of redemption, it sounded in the Apostles' word
of reconciliation, and it reverberated and goes on doing so in
the Bible.' What he says about the word of the cross could be
said of the rest of God's revelation. Forsyth speaks of the
Bible as the sacrament of God's present reality and power,

the word of God being in the Bible on its way to the soul. He is prepared to use the term 'infallibility', not in the sense that every sentence is infallible. 'The Bible's inspiration and its infallibility are such as pertain to Redemption and not theology, to Salvation and not mere history. It is as infallible as a Gospel requires.'

Early on in my ministry I was helped by two other evangelical theologians, James Orr and James Denney. Orr said,

> It is urged . . . that unless we can demonstrate what is called 'inerrancy' of the biblical record, down to even its minutest details, the whole edifice of belief in revealed religion falls to the ground. This, on the face of it, is a most suicidal position for any defender of revelation to take up . . . Such 'inerrancy' can never be demonstrated with any cogency which entitles it to rank as the foundation of a belief in inspiration.[5]

Denney is on record as follows:

> The infallibility of the Scriptures is not a verbal inerrancy or historical accuracy, but an infallibility of power to save. The word of God infallibly carries God's power to save. The word of God infallibly carries God's power to save men's souls. That is the only kind of infallibility I believe in. For a mere verbal inerrancy I care not one straw. It is worth nothing to me; it would be worth nothing if it were there, and it is not.[6]

I am encouraged that two recent books, published in 2003, generally accord with what Forsyth was saying nearly a century ago. John Webster writes:

> Revelation is the self-presentation of the triune God, the

free work of sovereign mercy in which God wills, establishes and perfects saving fellowship with himself in which
humankind comes to know, love and fear him above all
things . . . Theological talk of the inspiration of Scripture
needs to be strictly subordinate to and dependent upon
the broader concept of revelation. Disorder threatens a
theology of Scripture if the notion of inspiration is allowed
to aggrandise itself and usurp the central place in bibliog-
raphy. The disorder creeps in when the precise mode of
Scripture's production and, most of all, the role played by
the Holy Spirit in the inscripturation of revelation become
the hinges on which all else turns.[7]

John Webster is in no doubt that in revelation God makes
himself present in sovereign mercy and he is the agent, but
equally he is in no doubt about the creaturely reality of the
Scriptures. Neither their creatureliness nor their relationship
to God can be denied. Their creaturely realities are set apart,
sanctified by God to serve his self-presentation. What is
sanctified remains creaturely. Sanctification does not imply
transubstantiation

From the other book, *Reading the Bible Wisely* (SPCK) by
Richard Briggs I note,

(the) Bible we have is one that God was happy to leave
with us, copying errors, grammatical problems, historical
and ethical hard questions notwithstanding. The desire of
some to turn the Bible into the book that they would have
produced had they been in God's shoes, whether the 'they'
in question is on the left or the right of the theological
spectrum, needs to be resisted and seen for the dangerous
form of spiritual pride it often is.[8]

Problems alluded to by Dr Briggs will include discrepancies

in numbers in Old Testament documents and strict accuracy of stories of events. For instance, could Noah's Flood cover the whole earth and could representatives of every species – several millions in all – get into the Ark? Dogmatic claims to be unerringly correct in all interpretation and application of Scripture are relevant here. In the 1970s I wondered why evangelical commentaries would acknowledge problems raised by critical studies but there was no major work facing up to them. A scholar I know told me that a book of essays, edited by Howard Marshall, was about to appear in which he was a contributor – *New Testament Introduction* (1977). I understood that IVF had declined to publish it, but Paternoster Press had agreed.

In the editor's foreword Howard Marshall states:

> We have written as conservative evangelicals who combine a high regard for the authority of Scripture with the belief that we are called to study it with the full use of our minds . . . Belief in the 'truth' of the Bible cannot be a substitute for historical study. We may wish . . . that God had given us a Bible that would be instantly and correctly understandable by any modern man. But he has not done so, just as he has not given us a Bible with guaranteed text.[9]

I recall in earlier years the analogy of the incarnation to describe the nature of Scripture. As deity and humanity are perfectly blended in the incarnate Christ ensuring that he is in his humanity without sin and without error, so, it was said, there is a similar blend in Scripture. To me the analogy does not fit. Whatever the providential control in inspiration the humanity involved is neither perfect nor sinless. As John Webster maintains, the analogy of the hypostatic union if applied to Scripture militates against the uniqueness of the incarnation. Extension of the concept of incarnation to other aspects of God's economy of salvation is dangerous.

As in other areas of theology and practice to be dealt with later, evangelical positions were based more on opposition to those of other traditions, catholic or liberal, rather than careful search for the truth.

The Bible presents God's grand story. It has five chapters, as Tom Wright and others have shown – creation, the fall, the call of Israel, Jesus and the kingdom, the consummation in glory. Some would divide the fourth chapter and link the kingdom and the consummation as one chapter. It is important to recognize that there is both continuity and discontinuity between the chapters.

As a prelude to the subject of interpretation, I echo convictions convincingly presented by Forsyth in his great work, *The Person and Place of Jesus Christ*. The apostles' exposition of the act of God in Christ partakes of the finality of God's redemptive revelation. In matters more peripheral, however, such as their anthropology, and their connection of physical death with the Fall, and other matters, they reflect the culture and understanding of their time.

# 2

# Interpretation

All that has been said so far serves to emphasize the role of interpretation and application of Scripture. I attempt here no comprehensive sketch of the principles of interpretation. I simply draw attention to some factors I believe important as we recognize that biblical authority is the authority of the Bible rightly interpreted and applied.

The second NEAC at Nottingham issued 12 'Declarations of Intent'. Number 2 of the 12 was: 'We acknowledge that our handling of inspired and authoritative Scripture has often been clumsy and our interpretation of it shoddy, and we resolve to seek a more disciplined understanding of God's Holy Word.' Are we sure we are following out that intent in current controversies? As a warning about how mistaken interpretation can be, I recently read of members of a Free Church in the Western Isles seceding because their minister's wife gave birth on a Sunday. Because God had said 'Six days shalt thou labour' by going into labour on the Sabbath (!) she had earned God's disapproval. That may be an extreme example of misinterpretation, but church history can furnish many examples even by prominent leaders. Some will be mentioned later.

## The principle of development

Revelation in Scripture is a progressive revelation. In the Bible we see a unique educational process whereby progressive knowledge of God and his ways with and for humanity is imparted. It is always within the framework of human knowledge and understanding at the time. God reveals to his servants that amount of truth, and does it in such a way as they in that age can take. But what is newly revealed at any time bursts the existing framework of known truth, and when a new framework emerges, the relative and temporary aspects of revelation are left behind. This is true of all human processes of learning from infancy and through life. So, within Scripture itself partial concepts, expressed in anthropomorphic understanding of the times, are corrected by later and fuller revelation, or left behind.

In the Mosaic Law there are over 600 commandments not just 10. In the course of Jewish and Christian history many are left behind. The ceremonial and sacrificial laws are fulfilled and left behind in the sacrifice of Christ. But many of the social and moral commands are left behind, or modified, particularly those appropriate to life in the wilderness through 40 years. Capital punishment for adultery and homosexual activities as well as other criminal acts, health laws, notably relating to childbirth and women's bodily functions, and food laws are later disregarded. In respect of the latter it was by divine intervention through the teaching of Jesus and the vision to Peter on the house top that change came. Even the Ten Commandments have not been unaffected. The early Church changed the seventh day to the first, the Lord's resurrection day, on which it was no longer possible to 'do no manner of work', as Sunday was not a day of rest in the first century AD. Undoubtedly the first Christians as Jews observed the Sabbath as well, but the growing number of Gentiles did not. As for the fifth commandment I have yet to hear a preacher claiming that honouring of parents will guarantee a long life, though of course, the relevance originally is to Israel's occupation of the promised land. My point is the need for care in isolating phrases or words plucked out of context.

In short, there are aspects of revelation that are of a temporary significance. In the case of some, Scripture itself makes it clear, with others a developing Christian judgement leads to the same conclusion. Development of understanding of revelation is not confined to the biblical era. Understanding cannot be static through Christian history. A formal doctrine of the Trinity, though derived from Scripture, is a development. The famous dictum, 'God has ever more light to break forth from his Word', expresses the basis of development. A particular problem for many reading the Old Testament are the stories from the historical books in which Jehovah appears vindictive, advocating widespread slaughter. Without doubt a major purpose of the Lord's dealings with his people was to preserve a monotheistic faith in them, preserve them from contamination with pagan religions and inculcate a sense of his holiness. I find a growing number of Christians puzzled as to how to understand sections of the Old Testament, particularly the historical books. They ask how God speaks to them through such stories today. In some passages God appears to be less merciful than his servants, ordering slaughter and even devious actions. The cultural context in which these messages were received was such that they would seem reasonable and right The occupation and control of the Promised Land necessitated warfare. Reading these passages in our day requires recognition that the context has passed and thus what the Bible reveals there about God has to be seen in a later, different light. But how may Christians today get a fuller view of the God they serve? Only by turning to the cross of Christ and in that dying man, taking all the sin, rejection, hatred, injustice of the world into himself, can we see God as he is. This is our God. He achieves his saving purposes by self-sacrificing suffering love. Only by dying and rising does his kingdom get established and grow – by sacrificial love and grace rather than by military action.

## The principle of congruity

This is about the indivisibility of all truth. All truth is God's truth, so we must seek the congruity of all truth. We cannot be content to keep different aspects of truth in different compartments in the mind, scriptural truth, scientific truth, unrelated and unreconciled. I quote James Denney, another theologian of the past to whom I owe much:

> The doctrine of God, in the very nature of the case, is related to everything that enters into our knowledge; all our world depends on him, and hence it follows that a systematic presentation of the doctrine of God involves a general view of the world through God . . . All that man knows – God and the world – must be capable of being constructed into one coherent intellectual whole . . . The world is all of a piece, man's mind is all of a piece, and those easy and tempting solutions of our hardest problems, which either arrange the world or the activities of the mind in compartments, having no communications with each other, are simply to be rejected.[10]

An obvious application of this principle concerns the early chapters of Genesis. Without the assured facts of geology, astronomy, physics, genetics, discovered in modern times our knowledge of the universe, of this planet and the development of life, would be simplistically false. The literal approach of so-called creationists to the first three chapters of Genesis, while claiming to be honouring God's word does in fact undermine the credibility of the Bible's message. It blatantly ignores fact, reality, about the universe, and thus invites ridicule. Indeed, modern discovery has given a truer and fuller understanding of the biblical revelation of creation, and has, in fact, enriched our doctrine of creation. In other fields of human knowledge the same is true. In each generation Christians reflecting on the Scriptures within a context of current knowledge in all areas of life can make deductions for belief or behaviour or social action not contemplated by earlier generations. I believe this may well be true in current debates on sexuality.

A recent study of Richard Hooker reveals support for this approach to truth. Kenneth A. Locke writes: 'Hooker rejects the notion that scripture is and must be treated as the only source of human wisdom and knowledge. To limit oneself solely to the scriptures is to cut oneself off from the many other ways God imparts his will to humanity.'[11] Mark Noll quotes Jonathan Edwards, the outstanding mid-eighteenth-century evangelical, as maintaining that true knowledge was 'the consistency and agreement of our ideas with the ideas of God . . . all the arts and sciences, the more they are perfected, the more they issue in divinity, and coincide with it, and appear to be part of it.'[12] In this respect Christians must strive for intellectual integrity. Sloppy arguments to defend views believed to represent God's truth are to be shunned. In support of creationist convictions the claim of intelligent design to combat Darwinism is adduced. While it is reasonable to contend that the structure of the universe and a wonderful system of natural, physical laws supports the concept of a perfect Mind originating everything, there is much that cannot be by loving predetermined design – parasites in mosquitoes causing death by malaria for millions, deadly mutating viruses, babies born with incurable deformities, and so on, are examples.

I believe we must say that, though God is Creator he, in love, allowed his creation to develop itself. Love allows the loved one to be, to develop. As a nineteenth-century Christian leader put it, God could have made a perfect world. He did something more wonderful; he created a world that could make itself. As a way of emphasizing the need for intellectual integrity in relating biblical truth with truth known elsewhere I adduce astonishing claims recently made in a Christian periodical from Northern Ireland. They are by a man with a doctorate of some kind in seeking to affirm the literal, historic truth of the Genesis account of creation, Adam and Eve are said to have been created as mature adults, not as toddlers. Before the Fall he is said to have had a perfect brain, able to name all the animals created in the six days (nothing is said about creatures he never saw), whereas our brains have 'suffered from thousands of years of sin and the curse'. Indeed Adam's brain could store much more than today's computers, he maintains. The author tries to use science to back up his interpretation of Genesis. Soil scientists maintain it takes 300 to 1,000 years to produce naturally one inch of fertile soil. So, we may assume that a layer of six inches was needed in the Garden of Eden, taking between 1,800 and 6,000 years, but the soil was 'only a few days old with a superficial appearance of age'. All plants and animals were created mature, unspoiled by disease. God made 'chickens rather than eggs to hatch out into chickens'. It is this sort of argument that I believe brings Christians into disrepute.

We must reckon, I believe, with the fact that in communication of his revealed truth God does it in the context of the knowledge and understanding of the time. There could be a fuller and more important significance relating to a later stage of God's developing revelation than the human writer understands at the time. Some of the Old Testament prophecies later to be fulfilled in the Messiah's person and work are obvious examples. Reference to immediate developments which could be within the recipient's understanding carried with them deeper, more distinct meaning.

In New Testament writings also, however, we can recognize revelation being given in the context of current knowledge and understanding. This may be illustrated by examining the concept of death, particularly in Paul's letters. Three meanings of the word 'death' are apparent – physical death of the body, spiritual death in separation from God through sin, and what, for want of a better description, may be called behavioural death, the rejection of the unregenerate human nature by reason of baptism into Christ's death and resurrection. The 1662 Prayer Book speaks of 'dying from sin and rising again into righteousness, continually mortifying all our evil and corrupt affections'. In any context we need to ascertain which meaning is intended. It is not always easy to distinguish the first two meanings just referred to. In 1 Corinthians 15 both occur. In the well-known shout of victory, 'O death, where is thy sting, O grave, where is thy victory' physical death is clearly in mind. But then Paul says, 'The sting of death is sin'. Is he saying that physical death for human beings is a result of the sin we all share? There are verses in Romans 5 which tend to that understanding. Could it be that Paul is relying on Genesis 3 as an explanation of the entry of physical death into the human race? Eating of the fruit of the tree brings death. Adam and Eve are driven out of the garden lest they eat of the fruit of the tree of life 'and live forever'. There was no reason why Paul should not take these references as teaching that physical death has been brought about by sin. In the context of current understanding that would be natural.

In our modern understanding, however, we know that the cycle of birth, life, decay and death has prevailed from the beginning of the universe. Stars, planets, all vegetation, animate life and the human species share that cycle. Death reigned before ever humans sinned, before ever they emerged on the earth. We share the same bodily structure and functions as many other creatures. Decay leads to death.

If this illustration confirms the truth that all revelation is given within the context of understanding of the time, we need to see how it relates to Scripture in our interpretation. It also emphasizes that the writings are 'creaturely'.

## The principle of application

This principle refers to the need to relate the context in which some biblical truth was first given to the situation we are in, where it has to be applied. That original context may be vastly different from ours. The way we assess our situation has been shaped by many factors, within our own personality, history and social influences. The danger is of interpreting and applying Scripture in a way that owes more to our psychological needs and personal inclinations than to the Spirit's leading. I cannot avoid the conclusion that the various debates and divisions in the realm of sexuality have been unduly influenced by deep emotional proclivities on both sides. We need both humility and honesty to know ourselves as well as can be. It is true of all human beings that we are inclined to believe what we want to believe, and that applies to our approach to the Bible.

A cultural change from biblical times to today concerns the relationship of men and women. I will mention this again in dealing with the ordination of women. There can be no doubt that throughout the centuries in which the Scriptures were given society was patriarchal. It was undoubtedly a man's world. Man should be the head in the home, in the nation, in the religious life at any rate of God's people. Women should be in a submissive role. Was this God's revealed will for humanity, or just how life developed? Certainly in primitive societies the man would go out to provide sustenance, defend the family, and women would care for the home and the children she had borne. Did God accommodate his revelation to this or directly will it? Genesis 3 indicates that women would be subject to men. But it is important that this is presented as a consequence of sin rather than the ideal. It could well be argued that patriarchy was a consequence of humanity's fallen condition. Genesis 2 presents a picture of man created first and then woman as a helpmeet. But this is surely teaching religious truth about the complementary nature of marriage rather than historical fact or female submission. In any case the earlier creation story (Genesis 1.27) presents male and female together as in the image of God.

As we move on through Scripture we find exceptions to the male headship pattern. Deborah is raised up by God to lead his people and pretty authoritative she is. Huldah, a prophetess, is no weak, submissive female. She orders men. In the New Testament while Paul, and no doubt fellow apostles, took early chapters of Genesis as literal history, apparently, women leaders are evident without apostolic disapproval. Lydia becomes the leader of the first house-church in Europe. Priscilla appears to be equally prominent as her husband. Phoebe has at least a diaconal role, and among 'apostles' in Romans 16.7 is a female name, Junia. A crucial few verses, however, come in 1 Corinthians 11. Man is said to be head of the woman, as Christ is the head of man and God is the head of Christ. Paul, referring to Genesis 2, maintains that the priority of man in creation indicates that he, not woman, is in the image of God. This ignores Genesis 1.27 where both male and female are made in the image of God. Some commentators take 'head' in those verses to mean source not leadership, and I am convinced. The first use of 'head' in the Bible is to the head or source of a river. Paul obviously has the early chapters of Genesis in mind. In the Genesis 2 story the woman's source is in the man. In what sense is Christ the source of man? As the creating word of God, we could say. If, however, we attribute headship in the modern sense to God over Christ, what are the consequences for our doctrine of the Trinity? Whereas, if source is the concept we are reflecting the credal affirmation is that Christ is 'God of God', proceeding from the Father.

There is a challenging question to face in the context here. Paul, as already mentioned, apparently takes Genesis 2 as literal history, and bases theological exposition on it. But can we take creation of the male out of the dust of the earth and the female out of the rib of the male as historical truth rather than myth teaching some theological truth? Everything we now know of the human species, of genes, DNA and bodily structure testifies to evolution from earlier species. Almost 99 per cent of our genes are shared with other primates, and many of them with much more primitive forms of life. The human embryo begins with feminine chromosomes and later than conception the Y male factor kicks in for males. How, then, are we to interpret Paul's assertion that 'man was not created from woman, but woman from man'? We must face the fact that Paul is presenting what he sees as theological truth on the basis of his interpretation. I see the need here to recognize the creaturely nature of Scripture as emphasized by John Webster mentioned earlier. As it is necessary to understand the cultural context in interpreting the Old Testament passages, so it is true for New Testament writings. Attitudes to the institution of slavery, to appropriate behaviour in prevailing society, to man–woman relationships are examples.

We must recognize a reciprocal relationship between God and revelation and the current understanding in which the revelation is received.

The commentaries of F. F. Bruce and C. K. Barrett take 'head' to mean source. It is true there are few uses in Greek indicating source. But, though writing in Greek, Paul's mind was steeped in Hebrew thought and terminology. In Hebrew the directing centre of the personality was not in the head but in the heart and guts. *The New Bible Dictionary* (IVP, 1962) affirms: 'The head is not regarded as the seat of the intellect controlling the body, but as the source of life.'

In the first decades of the Church, as the gospel spread into the Gentile world, problems arose in men–women relationships in some congregations. Understandably, leadership was generally male, but women relishing a new liberty in Christ were inclined to exploit it in the worship sessions with resulting disorder. Was Paul not saying that distinctions between men and women no longer counted in Christ? There was now a new covenant between God and his people. So Paul had to be strict in injunctions to the church at Corinth. But both he and Peter were convinced that husbands have authority over wives, just as Christ has authority over the Church. In their letters they are emphatic on this matter. But then they are equally clear that women must not beautify themselves with jewellery, expensive dresses, hair styles, and must wear a veil in church covering their long hair and that men must not have long hair. How many women or men today take any notice of that? However critical I am of the fashion industry I cannot escape the conclusion that a great difference of culture between then and now exists. However appropriate their instructions as a word from the Lord were in their day, does the same word apply with equal force to us?

It can be argued that in the New Testament new truths

emerge from the new covenant in Christ which in time will lead to changes in society. An obvious example is the institution of slavery. In Christ there are neither bond nor free persons. Yet the institution prevailed throughout society. Nothing could be done in the first century to overturn it – nor for many centuries. Eventually some Christians with others of goodwill campaigned to end slavery. I have evidence from a descendant of Thomas Fowell Buxton that other Christians at the time opposed the abolition on the grounds that the Bible accepted slavery. The apostles, it was said, accepted the institution of slavery. He has his ancestor's papers to verify this.

To draw conclusions from difference in culture in Bible times and today is a slippery path. To set aside or moderate scriptural injunctions on grounds of culture is all too easy. But the task of recognizing new light in changed situations must be undertaken. If we can imagine two patterns printed on transparent material, so that one may be superimposed on the other, we may see where they correspond and where differ. Through interplay of the two we may with patience hear God's word for us, as clearly as those who heard it in biblical times. The Lord is the Lord of history, the Holy Spirit is given to the Church for all times to lead it into all truth. All must face the question whether the changed relationship between men and women in the last century or so affording a more fruitful partnership between the sexes, an emancipation, in fact, for many women to take their full part in society, national and civic affairs, education, medicine and industry, is of God or not. Inevitably, as in all change, there can be abuses and detrimental effects, but the overall benefits are to be assessed. In this far-reaching development in history the hand of God may be seen, not least in the Church. The Church is a sign and foretaste of God's kingdom in which differences of sex are at last irrelevant.

Faithful interpretation of Scripture in all its parts demands humility, patience, prayer. John Webster talks of a baptized reading of Scripture – reading that is mortified and vivified by the Holy Spirit. But of one thing we can be certain. God's way of salvation for humanity through Christ crucified and risen, his grand story from creation to final glory in heaven is clear and plain. John Wesley wanted one book to get him to heaven. He had it, so do we, but we must use it aright.

I do not deny the possibility of God in his sovereign purpose using our doubtful interpretation of Scripture to guide us in certain circumstances. A good friend of mine from college days used to tell of an incident in the Army during the war. He was, apparently, able to wangle a weekend's leave but uncertain whether he should do so. He was in a canteen eating a sausage roll, and happened to read an incident in the book of Ezekiel. The word came to the prophet – 'take this roll and go'! He thought it was God's guidance. Perhaps more seriously, when I joined the Navy at the age of 18 a great-aunt with long Christian experience gave me a verse from Scripture I was to hang on to. Genesis 28.15 says, 'I will keep you in all places wherever you go, and I will bring you back to this land.' Those words I took as a promise to me as to Jacob. And whether I was using Scripture aright I did in fact experience God's protection in circumstances that could easily have proved fatal. We can believe that in his long-suffering grace God can accommodate himself to our imperfections and limited understanding. He certainly does not make our salvation and acceptance with him depend on perfect interpretation of Scripture or doctrinal orthodoxy. Let evangelicals bear that in mind when they oppose the interpretations of other Christians.

# 3

# The Church

If asked in my earlier years, 'What is the nature of the Church?' the reply would be, 'The company of all those, known only to God, who have been converted and born again.' It was the mystical, and invisible Body of Christ. Not all by a long way of those belonging to the outward form of the Church, the institutional Church, were in the true Church. The positive truth in that position cannot be denied. It is clearly possible to attend church, receive the sacraments, even serve its structures, and have no living relationship with God through trust in Christ. But I have long come to recognize that it is a serious mistake to denigrate the visible, institutional Church continuing through the ages. The Church is the sign, instrument and foretaste of God's kingdom. A sign has to be seen, observed in the world. An instrument has to be actively employed in the world. And a foretaste of what the kingdom in all its fullness in heaven is going to be like must be observable. The Church is not just a divinely created company, known only to God, but is a human institution with all its virtues and faults. If the world is to believe, as Jesus prayed before his crucifixion, his believers must be *seen* as a loving community.

As the Archbishop of Canterbury has recently maintained, Jesus was not in his teaching occupied with the structural organization of an institutional Church. His message was about the kingdom of God and the establishment of relationships in God's will. He did declare that on the confession of Peter concerning his messiahship and commitment to himself he would build his Church. At that stage his *Ecclesia* would be understood as an association of those with faith in him. Before his crucifixion he promised that the holy Spirit would guide his followers 'into all truth'. That certainly would include the understanding of all that his death and resurrection would achieve. But we must surely believe that the Holy Spirit, who could 'abide with his Church forever', would also lead in the development of its form in the world as a human as well as a divine institution once it was clear to the early Christians that the parousia was not immediately imminent. And before long some organization became evident, at first in local assemblies of believers. Pastoral care, teaching ministry and administration of the sacraments required some agreed order. And, as distortions of the primitive gospel and heresies began to emerge, a way of safeguarding orthodoxy had to be found, once the apostles were dead. Hence developed episcopal oversight and leadership, adherence to the faith and practice of the Church being by communion with the bishop. Because all believers remain sinful and fallible creatures, infallibility of the Church could never be guaranteed.

Every effort to make the Church visible coterminous with the Church mystical – to delineate as a 'pure' church – is bound to fail. To circumscribe membership and fence round the sacraments for true believers is contrary to scriptural standards.

In Old Testament history there were periods when apostasy was widespread. Yet none of the prophets advocated withholding of circumcision, the mark of God's covenant. Severe judgements fell on the faithless and rebellious, and there was condemnation of insincere approach to worship and the sacrificial system. But the authority for the worship, sacrifices and circumcision was not withdrawn. After Pentecost, although it would take some time for the Church's institutional form to settle down under the Spirit's guidance, baptism was administered widely without, apparently, prolonged preparation. Within a brief span thousands were baptized. The Philippian jailor and all his household were baptized in the middle of the night after his own profession of faith. Not everyone who received baptism could have turned out to be lifelong disciples of Christ. These considerations weigh with me in respect of attempts to impose a very tight baptismal policy in parishes. I am not for a careless lack of preparation, but in the end we cannot make 'windows into men's souls', as Elizabeth I put it. As communicants kneel at the communion rails, who would dare to question each one if they were truly penitent, trusting Christ and in love and charity with their neighbours, before administering the elements? This is not to say that discipline should not be exercised where known sin is not being forsaken.

I much regret an apparent failure among evangelicals to appreciate the catholicity of the Church, its historic heritage and development over the centuries. I appreciate the concern to be relevant and contemporary, 'anchored to the Rock but geared to the times' (to quote a motto from some decades ago), but not at the expense of what the past has made us Anglican evangelicals in the twenty-first century. I accept Michael Ramsey's emphasis on the provisionality of Anglicanism. We exist for what in God's purposes the Church will become. But I believe the emergence of a Church episcopally led was under the Spirit's guidance. This is not to say that non-episcopal churches are not in the apostolic succession of faith, order and mission. It is right, however, in my view that a uniting of separated churches should be within a reformed episcopacy sensitively arranged. Although relatively modern in its formulation the Chicago-Lambeth Quadrilateral, affirming Scripture, the creeds, the dominical sacraments and the episcopacy, is the right basis for union. In purely pragmatic terms I would as a minister rather be under the authority of one person, a bishop, than a committee. Committees can be faceless and shirk personal responsibility.

Individual clergy and congregations have sometimes not seen eye to eye with their bishop. Indeed though called to be a guardian of the truth they have accused him (or now her) of departing from the truth. In the current controversies over homosexual practices in the ranks of the clergy some evangelicals have been rejecting the ministry of their bishop, as some Anglo-Catholics have rejected that ministry because of the ordination of women priests. On the one hand the bishop has been judged as rejecting the authority of Scripture, on the other hand rejecting Catholic order. Adherence to the truth as one perceives it, especially in one's tradition and as held for a long time, is not to be condemned. But it can lead to stubborn pride and defending one's convictions at all costs if they serve a sense of security. The result can be unwillingness to enter charitable dialogue, the basis of which must be the recognition that the other partner is seeking the truth. It is hard to imagine anyone staying with the Church with all its problems and pressures unless concerned with the truth.

I am generally happy, as I would think are most evangelicals, with the Articles of Religion. Article 26 states that because the visible Church has 'evil' mingled with 'good', sometimes the 'evil have chief authority in the Ministration of the word and sacraments'. Yet because ministers do not minister in their own name but in Christ's and by his commission and authority, we may use their ministry both in hearing the Word of God and in receiving the Sacraments. Nor is the grace of God's gifts diminished by the wickedness of the ministers. It would be a shameful calumny to charge bishops who disagree with one's position, say, on an interpretation of Scripture with 'wickedness'. In the case of those deemed guilty of wickedness the Article advocates inquiry of those accused and if found guilty there is liability to be deposed. An ecclesiastical court is presupposed.

As disagreement in understanding God's will on any matter does not lie in the realm of wickedness, what should be the way of attempting reconciliation? It should be in unhurried charitable debate, not in rejecting the other's ministry. I believe the intransigence of some evangelicals in their attitude to their bishops, and to others in the Church who differ from them, is in the long run detrimental to their witness. Their assumption that they have the full grasp of God's will, an incontrovertible interpretation of Scripture, shows a lack of humble acknowledgement that there may be more of God's truth to discover. No doubt there will be protest that they are simply upholding the authority of Scripture, but I would emphasize in response the need for clearer thinking on the way God's authority is expressed through Scripture. There is much to support this view in the writings of evangelical theologians.

As well as rejecting their bishop's ministrations, some clergy and congregations threaten to withhold financial contributions to the diocesan budget. I cannot avoid regarding this as financial blackmail. They are saying, 'Agree with us or forfeit our financial support!' Apart from the diocesan budget contributing largely to clergy stipends and pensions, which such clergy are happy to receive, it also provides for ministry across the diocese to the community in education, social concerns, ecumenical relationships, selection of ordained and lay ministry. No single parish can perform all the ministry and mission needed across a wide area in conurbations or rural areas. Then there are the contributions each diocese makes to the national structures of the Church of England. As the established Church it has national responsibilities, not just to the dioceses in areas like the Board of Ministry and in providing resources of various kinds, but with other churches serving the nation. I realized from 25 years on General Synod and its Standing Committee that on complex ethical issues governments expect well-informed input from the Church of England, and because we cover every square yard of England, and act for the State on some matters, such as marriages, parliament becomes concerned from time to time in our affairs.

A basic failing, in my judgement, of many evangelicals, clergy and laity, is lack of a clear ecclesiology. At NEAC 3 in Caister in 1987 the Archbishop of Canterbury, Robert Runcie, at the instigation of certain evangelicals, challenged us to review and develop our ecclesiology. We have largely failed to meet that challenge, probably because the gospel is regarded as more important than the doctrine of the Church. Yet the Church is part of the gospel. Believers are by baptism incorporated into the Church, the Body of Christ. No evangelical would deny that. Yet many operate on a congregationalist basis rather than an Anglican. To hold a congregationalist understanding of church order is obviously an honoured and worthy tradition. The United Reformed Church, the continuing Congregationalist churches, the Presbyterian, the Baptist, Pentecostal churches, the Brethren and the Fellowship of Independent Evangelical Churches are all in that tradition. The local congregation orders its affairs, they maintain, under the lordship of Christ. Anglicans, inheriting historic, catholic order, as confirmed at the Reformation, see the local church as a fellowship of congregations in communion with their bishop. One cannot escape the feeling that some evangelical congregations would be more at home in the Fellowship of Independent Evangelical Churches. The attraction would be they could conduct their affairs entirely as they would wish, spend their money as they wish, be completely free in conduct of worship and have their own arrangements for supporting their ministers. It has some attraction, especially for strong congregations. Anglican ordained ministry is by a bishop in the historical succession. Through him authority is conferred, and with him the 'cure of souls' is shared. Anglicans, including many evangelicals, are content to stay with that understanding. I warmly welcome the appearance of a new journal entitled *Ecclesiology*. I have found its early editions most helpful. I hope it will stimulate evangelical debate.

Authority cannot be exercised in the Church solely by bishops. One reason I could not be a Roman Catholic is because as yet it has not escaped from that form of authority. In its exercise authority must embrace bishops, other clergy and laity. Even in apostolic times this was so. The first council of the Church to decide a fundamental question on the gospel – the Council of Jerusalem (Acts 15.5–29) – was not just a meeting of the apostles. And when Paul had to deal with difficult problems in the church at Corinth he gave his firm view but he called on the members of the Church to decide with him. Some of those members were probably from the slave section of the community but they were trusted to act.

At the Reformation bishops and convocation of clergy continued, but the king and parliament shared in authority as representatives then of the laity. When the American colonies broke away from British rule Anglicans were faced with a problem of authority, with the removal of royal powers. They ensured, however, that episcopal leadership should be complemented and in council with clergy and lay representation. It is said that those who drew up the American constitution of the two houses, the Representatives and the Senate, crossed the road and established the Episcopal Church of the United

States of America with a house of bishops and a house of deputies of clergy and laity – the first instance of Anglican episcopal leadership and synodical government. The next church outside Britain to adopt the pattern was that of New Zealand. And now every one of the 38 autonomous churches in the Communion is episcopally led and synodically governed. The Church of England came late into full expression of the principle in 1970. What is true of national churches is also true of the dioceses, and should be recognizably true of parishes. A church council should be a true partnership of clergy and laity under the episcopal care of the bishop. In Anglicanism we are not congregationalist in ecclesiology.

At the present time there is much confusion and ill-thought-out expression of what communion is. For some it is alliance with those Christians who agree with their detailed understanding of the faith and the behaviour that must go with it. Denominational boundaries are secondary to this alliance. Evangelicals holding this view put it all down to a correct understanding of Scripture. It is a matter of biblical authority. Turning to the Bible, one of the clearest statements on communion is in Ephesians 4. In his appeal for Christian behaviour and unity Paul bases it on, 'one Lord, one Faith, one Baptism'. So, if Christians acknowledge one Lord, the God revealed in Jesus Christ, share the faith rooted in the incarnation, death and resurrection of Christ, and are baptized in the name of the Trinity, they are in communion. Further reflection on the faith is required. What would Paul mean by it as he wrote his letter? As far as we can tell no formal creed goes back to apostolic times. The so-called Apostles' Creed is probably second century. So the 'Faith' in Ephesians must be belief, trust in Jesus Christ as Saviour and Lord, or at the most the truths preached about him. It is possible that for baptism the confession that Jesus is Lord could suffice.

I am firmly committed to the Anglican understanding of communion as it has been articulated over the last century or two. From the Reformation in England it has turned against the Roman Catholic tradition of defining how communion is achieved, namely by submission to the Pope. Whether the Reformers fully realized the implications at the time, they were turning their backs on a centralized juridical exercise of authority. Rather than centralization they adopted a dispersed understanding of authority. In the current divisions across the Anglican Communion some primates have been calling for increased powers for the Archbishop of Canterbury to exercise discipline against provinces or dioceses they judge to be denying the teaching of the Bible. I do not believe such a development will be acceptable to the Communion as a whole.

A second factor to be recognized is that Anglicanism is not a confessional church unlike other churches that emerged in the sixteenth century. Even the 39 Articles, for all their historic significance and value, have never been accepted as a confession of faith throughout the Communion. In wide areas of the Communion they have never appeared in any constitutional document and no subscription to them has been required. In a resolution of the 1968 Lambeth Conference, supported by all but a small minority of bishops, it was agreed that assent to the Articles should no longer be required of ordinands, and where it is required it should be given only in the context of a statement covering the full range of our inheritance of the faith, including the Ordinal and Book of Common Prayer indicating their historical context. The Church of England has now followed that direction.

In the face of the divisions the Communion has been experiencing, however, first over women priests, then women bishops and now ordination of practising homosexuals, what can be said about the way ahead? I would highlight a truth that seems to be generally overlooked. Anglicanism believes in a Church travelling light. At the Anglican Congress in Canada in 1963, Bishop Stephen Bayne, the first Executive Officer of the Anglican Communion said:

> A second great tradition of Anglican action is that we shall travel light – that we shall remember that we are a pilgrim people, and that a pilgrim carries with him [sic] only those things that are essential to his life. It is a characteristic mark of the Anglican tradition, at our best, that we recognise how few and how important the essentials are.[13]

That principle is abundantly illustrated in the Chicago/Lambeth Quadrilateral of 1886/1888:

A. The Holy Scriptures of the Old and New Testaments 'as containing all things necessary for salvation', and as being the rule and ultimate standard of faith.

B. The Apostles' Creed as the Baptismal Symbol; and the Nicene Creed as the sufficient statement of the Christian Faith.

C. The two Sacraments ordained by Christ himself – Baptism and the Supper of the Lord – ministered with unfailing use of Christ's words of Institution, and the elements ordained by Him.

D. The Historic Episcopate, locally adapted in the methods of its administration to the varying needs of the nations and people called of God into the Unity of His Church.[14]

The fourth point has occasioned some controversy over the following years. An attempt to modify it to meet some misgivings was made at Lambeth 1968, but with not much success. However we have to define the actual exercise of episcopal leadership and authority it remains an Anglican conviction that for full expression of the universal Church episcopacy is needed. Anglicans believe the early Church was rightly led in developing the concept and practice.

It must be emphasized how far short of a full confession the Quadrilateral is. There is no attempt to define doctrine beyond the statements of the two creeds mentioned. Nothing is said about the ways Scripture is to be interpreted and applied, though all are directed to it as the rule and standard of faith.

The consequences of travelling light with such a charter is that diversity within unity can be expected and lived with, however much it may upset those with convictions that they have incontrovertible grasp of the truth on disputed matters. I wonder if Christians today recognize the degree of diversity in the New Testament, not on the basic truth of salvation through grace by faith in Christ crucified and risen, but in approaches to revealed truth. One of the encouraging developments in the Church of England, for instance, is the tolerance now evident between traditions in the understanding of the sacraments. We are one by virtue of uniting in the same Lord's Supper, though perceptions of how the grace is conveyed and received may be quite different. At one time fierce controversies could result in refusal to join at the same table. 'We being many – with different convictions – are one Body' might be said now.

A further factor is the way culture affects our apprehension of the truth. Experience throughout the Communion impressed that truth on me. A trivial example! At Lambeth 1998 a previous book of mine had just appeared. Its title was *Debtor to Grace* – a concept that means much to me, taken from the hymn, 'O to grace how great a debtor daily I'm constrained to be'. A bishop from the African continent took me to task. How could I justify being in debt? To him being in debt, as his country was, was shameful and a situation to be remedied. More seriously, in some parts of the Communion, talk about deliverance into the liberty of the children of God means something different from its meaning for Christians in this country. There it is about the good news of God's deliverance from the slavery of poverty and injustice. On matters of sexuality there are different approaches influenced to some extent by culture.

Unity in diversity will be hard to achieve, but it is worth every effort, not least for the sake of the contribution of the Anglican Communion to the universal Church. Certainly the more we move towards unity with other Christians the more must we abandon any imposition of conformity and embrace diversity.

As long ago as Lambeth 1948 a report on the Anglican Communion faced the question, 'Is Anglicanism based on a sufficiently coherent form of authority to form the nucleus of a world-wide fellowship of Churches, or does its comprehensiveness conceal internal divisions which may cause its disruption?'[15] In answer the report maintained that former Lambeth Conferences have wisely rejected proposals for a formal primacy of Canterbury, for an appellate tribunal, and for giving the Conference the status of a legislative synod. So there was a repudiation of centralized government, and a refusal of a legal basis of union. The authority which binds the Communion together, therefore, is moral and spiritual, resting on the truth of the gospel, and on a charity that is patient and willing to defer to the common mind.

The report continues with the assertion that authority, as inherited from the undivided Church of the early centuries, is single in that it is derived from a single divine source, the Trinity, and reflects within itself the richness and historicity of the divine revelation. That authority is distributed among Scripture, tradition, creeds, the ministry of word and sacraments, the witness of saints and the *consensus fidelium*. It is thus a dispersed rather than a centralized authority. Its elements together contribute by a process of mutual support, mutual checking and redressing of errors or exaggerations to the fullness of authority committed by Christ to his Church. It is recognized that authority of this kind is much harder to understand and obey than authority of a more imperious character. The authority of Scripture is established because it is the unique and classical record of God's revelation in relation to and dealings with humanity. The report testifies to Scripture as the ultimate standard of faith but maintains the need for its continual interpretation in the context of the Church's life. The title of the report to that Conference is 'The Meaning and Unity of the Anglican Communion'.

In October 2004 the Windsor Report, by the Lambeth Commission on Communion, was published. It should be recognized for what it is not. It is not an attempt to resolve finally the issue underlying the current divisions in the Communion. I see its conclusions as reflecting the main thrust of that earlier report almost 60 years ago. How the Church should deal with homosexual relationships, and in particular their acceptance in the ranks of the ordained clergy, especially bishops, and their recognition by services of blessing is not resolved. I have no doubt that such a study is long overdue. The 1998 Lambeth Conference resolution on the subject plainly indicated that the debate was not concluded and urged that the primates and the ACC should take responsibility for its continuance.

In the year 2005, as a response to the threats of division and breakdown of communion in Anglicanism, some churches in the global South put forward their own basis for communion in the Church, maintaining wrongly that we are a confessional church. They declared that communion was dependent on agreement on the historic, apostolic faith.

What they failed, apparently, to recognize was that the faith could be expressed in different ways. Some would express it as salvation by grace through faith in Jesus Christ, crucified and risen, through whose subsitutionary sacrifice we are justified. Others would express it in the proclamation of the kingdom by which God establishes his rule in individual lives and through them works for justice and peace in society, feeding the hungry, clothing the naked, freeing captives of all kinds, as Jesus and the Old Testament prophets insisted. Others would claim it is the inauguration of the new covenant people of God and growth through baptism into Christ, the Church being identified and sustained in eucharistic participation in the body and blood of Christ. Each expression could be justified from Scripture. To comprehend all would demand a massive confession.

It is important to recognize, however, that underlying the homosexual issue is the more basic question of how we are to know God's will for the Church today. Scripture has a pivotal role, as the 1948 statement maintains, but it has need for continual interpretation in the context of the Church's life. On a range of matters interpretation has developed over 2,000 years. Christians have the right and the duty to express firmly their conclusions on disputed matters but, as St Paul says in Ephesians 4, they should be 'always humble, gentle, patient, tolerant to one another, doing their best to preserve the unity that binds us together'. That unity, as has already been mentioned, is by commitment to one Lord, one faith, one baptism.

Monolithic unity and uniformity will never be achieved in Anglicanism or in the wider universal Church. If one considers the universe with all its complexity, nature as we see it on this planet, the diversity of peoples throughout history, the individuality of all human persons, it would seem contrary to God's working out of his purposes for the Church to be entirely uniform. Heaven alone will bring complete harmony and mutual understanding of God's people.

The Windsor Report rightly endorses the autonomy of the 38 member churches. But it also corrects a present imbalance by stress on the interdependence essential for communion. As I shall emphasize later, the contribution of Anglicanism to the universal Church demands a unified approach. Interdependence is a required commitment both from America and Canada and the churches of the global South. To this end the proposal for an Anglican Covenant should be warmly received and implemented.

I welcome the report's proposals for clearer definition of the relationships between the Lambeth Conference, the Primates' Meeting and the ACC. After the 1988 Lambeth Conference there was some attention to this matter, and an issue arose when the primates and the ACC came to conflicting decisions. The matter was resolved by the ACC giving way. As a result the next meeting of the ACC was a joint meeting with the full Primates' Meeting. It proved unsatisfactory, but from then on the standing committees of both have met jointly.

The Archbishop of Canterbury has a unique role in the Communion. Member churches define themselves as being in communion with the See of Canterbury. He acts as president to the three consultative bodies, and he calls the bishops to the Lambeth Conference, with the implication that it is by his invitation. While hoping the Communion will resist anything like papal powers I welcome discussion as to how he may better relate to member churches for the avoidance of disunity. A council of advice, recognized by the churches, would be helpful. Indeed that is what the joint standing committees have been at various times.

In the New Testament, for all baptized Christians a way of life consistent with that profession was essential. If any individual was judged to be blatantly departing from that way of life they had to disciplined, regarded as out of fellowship until they repented. There appear to be no instances of whole congregations ruled out of fellowship or communion, or any necessity for it. There is a lot wrong with the seven churches in Revelation, but no suggestion as yet they are excluded. In so far as all this has relevance to the current situation in the Anglican Communion it seems to me we can distinguish between individuals and churches. No Anglican church, no diocese, has formally denied the Lordship of Christ, repudiated faith in him as Saviour, or abandoned baptism. No Church has chosen to reject any of the four points of the Lambeth Quadrilateral – Bible, creeds, dominical sacraments and episcopacy – Anglicanism's minimal basics of communion. Questions of interpretation continue to cause tension, but that is no new phenomenon. Baptismal controversies in the nineteenth century, the Colenso affair and split in South Africa, polygamy disputes in Africa, the ordination of women, are just some of the crises faced in Anglicanism. In the eighteenth century leadership in the Church of England was much influenced by Deism, a greater threat to the historic faith than most controversies today. Bishops could be said to be forsaking the faith once delivered to the saints. The Church did not split. God had his own way of dealing with the matter. He inspired the Evangelical Revival. Many bishops opposed it and eventually the Methodist Church was born. But now we feel driven to seek reconciliation and healing of division in this connection and wider afield. In the creed we say we believe in the one, holy, catholic, apostolic Church. While evangelicals may mentally connect that statement with the mystical, invisible Church, they should recognize its relevance to the institutional Church.

I believe that Anglicanism has a unique contribution to make to the worldwide Church. It represents Catholicism renewed by the Reformation and influenced by subsequent movements, notably the Enlightenment and the Romantic movement, and by the evangelical, catholic and liberal traditions. As with all movements in the history of the Church, there can be both beneficial and baneful effects, temporary and more lasting results. The Anglican Consultative Council in 1984 sought to define the Anglican ethos thus:

> The Communion seeks to be loyal to the apostolic faith and to safeguard and express it in Catholic order always to be reformed by the standards of Scripture. It allows for a responsible freedom and latitude of interpretation of the faith within a fellowship committed to the living expression of that faith.

It went on to emphasize the commitment to Reformed Catholicism and 'a way of thinking and feeling that has developed over the centuries which calls for an acceptance of measures of diversity, an openness, tolerance and mutual respect for others'. If I am asked why I am an Anglican, the answer is there stated. Indeed, my 15 years on the Anglican Consultative Council only served to strengthen that conviction.

There are two areas in particular where a united Communion is needed – mission and ecumenical relations. Mission comprehends evangelism, church planting, action for peace and justice and care of the environment. In 1984, at the sixth meeting of the ACC, a report of a working group on mission issues and strategy, set up by the ACC, was received. It began: 'Though there are notable exceptions, the dominant model of the Church within the Anglican Communion is a pastoral one. Emphasis in all aspects of the Church's life tends to be placed on care and nurture rather than proclamation and service'.[16] A shift of emphasis was called for. The

Church's task was 'making known the truth about God revealed in Christ through what Christians say, what they are and what they do'. In response the ACC at that meeting presented a definition of mission in four clauses:

1  To proclaim the good news of the kingdom
2  To teach, baptize and nurture the new believers
3  To respond to human needs by loving service
4  To seek to transform unjust structures of society.

It represents a convergence of previously narrow and conflicting attitudes to mission, as I had witnessed on my early days on the Church of England's Board for Mission and Unity. A study failing to seek convergence was rejected by the Board and I was invited to chair a new working group, whose report, 'Evangelism and the Mission of the Church' was well received.

In 1990, at the eighth meeting of the ACC, a fifth clause was added to the earlier definition:

5  To strive to safeguard the integrity of creation and sustain and review the life of the earth.[17]

The definition has been accepted and valued widely across the Communion. It constitutes an example of the Communion worldwide helping its member churches and dioceses. The work of no single diocese or voluntary organization would have commanded such attention. Throughout the Communion, resources for mission, in constructive thinking, personnel and finance, have been greatly increased through the Partners-in-Mission Consultations established by the ACC. To have Anglican partners come and review critically but sympathetically how a province or diocese is carrying out mission has proved very valuable. In matters of peace and justice individual areas have been much helped by member-ship and help from the Communion. A united Communion is needed for these benefits to continue.

The area of ecumenical relations also needs united thought and action. If the Roman Catholic Church, the various Orthodox Churches, the Methodists and the Lutherans want to relate to Anglicans, to know what they stand for or desire in the search for unity, a united Communion response is vital. Because Anglicanism is a comprehensive expression of what church is, ecumenical partners sometimes express puzzlement as to where we stand. That makes informed and theologically competent co-operation across the world and ecclesiological traditions of Anglicanism imperative.

It is careful consideration of concerns like these that those threatening division in the Communion – and over matters that come down to interpretation of Scripture of a particu-larly secondary nature – should ponder.

Over 20 years ago Bishop John Howe, then Secretary-General of the Anglican Consultative Council stated the need for the Communion to have some way of defining the limits within which churches of the Anglican Communion could remain in full communion.[18] While there was a mechanism for welcoming new members, provinces, into communion by votes of the Primates' Meeting and the ACC, there was no provision for expelling any member. An attempt was made to devise such a provision in the late 1980s but it came to nought, mainly because some churches feared loss of their autonomy. If such a provision is desired and possible it should not be a decision made solely by bishops or primates and certainly not by individual provinces, dioceses or parishes taking unilateral action. In the pattern of synodical procedures the ACC, bringing together bishops, clergy and laity, should also be involved. The attempt in the 1980s was based on the Chicago/Lambeth Quadrilateral illustrated by some Lambeth Conference resolutions that had in the light of subsequent history proved of lasting value.

Maintenance of the evangelical witness in Anglicanism has been a natural concern since the eighteenth century. Societies, fellowships and periodicals have served this end. In unity has been strength, it has seemed, even if it has not always been easy to maintain. One system on which reliance has been placed is patronage in appointment to parishes. Evangelical trusts, either of societies, groups or individuals, have sought to ensure a succession of evangelical clergy in parishes and even an introduction into other parishes. The rationale was that fellow-evangelicals rather than diocesan bodies or bishops could guarantee the right appointments. In the 1960s there was prolonged debate in the Church about clergy deployment and appointment. Patronage bodies were alarmed. Were their powers to be diminished or even abolished? In my first years on the General Synod from 1970 I found myself on the Terms of Ministry Committee required to consider new ways. I came to the conclusion that patronage bodies had too much power. The rights of the laity of a parish had little or no part in the process of appointing its clergy. I could not imagine any congregation in apostolic times having no say in appointment of their elders or presbyters. In 1969 I wrote a booklet, *Patronage Reformed for the 70s* in which a parish appointment system was suggested. A small body consisting of someone from the existing patronage body, if still existing, a representative of the bishop of the diocese and two parish representatives would act. Although in the course of events something similar was presented to the Synod it was not taken up. Patronage influences prevailed. There was some personal satisfaction a few years later when two parishes I had were united, and under the terms of the existing pastoral measure we removed the two relevant patronage bodies and substituted an ad hoc committee of bishop's representative, two representatives from the uniting parishes and a person from outside the diocese from the General Synod. At each vacancy fresh appointments were to be made.

I firmly believed that in the spirit of full participation in the Church of England stemming from NEAC 1 at Keele in 1967 the parish and diocese should be in partnership in clergy appointments. Trust could only be built up by exercising it. There is an interesting sidelight on this from a time spent on the Committee of the Bible Churchmen's Missionary Society. Since it was an evangelical missionary society there had been insistence of placing missionaries in dioceses overseas only where the Society at home decided. Then came a decisive development. The diocese of Central Tanganyika, then so named, had an evangelical bishop, Alfred Stanway from CMS Australia. Could BCMS agree to let him place our missionaries? He was, after all, 'one of us'. By a majority decision he was given that right, but some opposed it as a step down a slippery slope. The next thing would be to give such powers to a bishop who was not an evangelical! Nowadays no such fearful inhibitions prevail. I record this instance to illustrate how far evangelicals have moved – or, at least, most of them – and what I strongly believe about full participation in the Church at all levels. Co-operation in many ways with churchmen and parishes of other traditions is so much more widespread and fruitful than when I was ordained in 1951, and I rejoice in it.

No reflection on evangelical life in the Church of England should fail to mention the Charismatic Movement. In the analysis mentioned in the Introduction charismatic evangelicals were described as the third tradition, characterized by 'vitality and energy'. My own knowledge of the kind of renewal the movement represents goes back to my earliest years. The Pentecostal renewal originating in America reached Britain within a few years. One of the first places to be affected was my home town, Preston, around the time of World War One. Several of my father's relatives left the Church of England and joined the Assemblies of God church then formed. Relations between those continuing Church of England and members who had moved over remained good. In my mid-teens I occasionally visited the assembly with a school-friend. For the first time I witnessed speaking in tongues as part of worship. I noticed that it was predominantly the women who took part, there was very little interpreting of the utterances, and the leader of the session decided when to bring it to an end.

The General Synod in the 1970s began to take an interest in the Charismatic Movement in the Church of England, consequent upon the renewal, accompanied by glossolalia, in some parishes. The Standing Committee convened a consultation in 1979, widely representative of the Church of England, with guests. On its recommendation a working group to assess the movement was set up, which I was asked to chair. Its report was presented in 1981. Almost inevitably the consequent debate revealed a mixture of reactions.

Meanwhile the whole Anglican Communion was experiencing the spread of this particular kind of renewal, as were other churches, including the Roman Catholic, and Pentecostal churches were probably the fastest growing. In 1981 at the fifth meeting of the ACC, but not for the first time, consideration was given to the effects of the movement. Members with first-hand experience shared knowledge of benefits and problems. All member churches were asked to report on their experience of spiritual renewal including the charismatic. By ACC-6 (Nigeria, 1984) only five of the (then) 27 churches had replied. The ACC Standing Committee then decided to launch a book of essays on renewal, which I was asked to edit. Twelve essays from the various spiritual traditions in Anglicanism, including the charismatic, were published in 1987 under the title *Open to the Spirit*.[19] They reveal a wide range of responses.

From my earliest years, therefore, I have known of the Pentecostal/charismatic tradition. While I have learned to appreciate the benefits, I have not been able to get on board, so to speak. I gladly recognize the major renewal the movement has brought to many congregations and individual lives. There is vitality and enthusiasm where there was dull formality. Every-member ministry has become a reality. The ministry of healing has received a new emphasis, though this has also happened outside the movement. New forms of worship have been created, among them new worship songs, some of which I have been glad to share, even if others have seemed shallow in truth and ephemeral. It has meant that for many people the emotional content in worship has had freer rein. I appreciate that for many folk formal Anglican worship hardly touched the emotions, it was too cerebral. But vital worship should harmonize mind, will and emotions, and indeed possible bodily reactions. The latter were quite natural in Old Testament worship. Dance was considered appropriate. And though dance in worship does nothing for me, it obviously is a valued activity for some. Perhaps I have been inclined to be too cerebral in worship, but growing older I am deeply moved in singing some Wesley and Watts hymns, and some modern ones, like 'The Servant King'. In short, there has been a fuller and more effective recognition of the work of the Holy Spirit in the life and mission of the Church. The largely unknown third person of the Trinity has had room to do what Jesus said he would be given to do.

What, then restrains me from being fully committed to the movement? For one thing, I cannot follow the way the baptism of the Spirit is taught. It is not for me a distinct and separate baptism. I take it that all the Spirit has for us is pledged in the one baptism into the Trinity, although little may be known or experienced at the time of that initial rite, especially, of course, if administered in childhood. New experiences, even profound and life-altering experiences may subsequently occur at the Spirit's initiative, and more than once. But I do not feel convinced I should seek a once-for-all baptism of the Spirit.

Nor do I believe that glossolalia is a required gift and necessary evidence of the Spirit's full control. For those who find it a rich medium of worship of God I am glad. I am also hesitant about claims of prophecy. It is all too easy for individuals, whether charismatic or not, to claim a direct word from God. To claim a word of prophecy no doubt enhances self-esteem, but how often Christians have declared that God has told them of some course of action, which has proved to be sadly mistaken. Individual guidance is undoubtedly both possible and from God, but generally needs testing with other Christians. In a congregation an individual may claim to have a word of prophecy. Others may feel it is more in accordance with God's will to have a consultation of a number of members in unhurried prayer and reflection. The latter way is no less evidence of the Spirit's working.

Over the years I have come to believe that a basic question about spirituality is, what am I looking for? Is it really a spiritual 'feel-good' factor? In an age of materialism and hedonism there is evidence of spiritual hunger. In this post-modern age people are encouraged to follow what 'works for them', there being no absolute authorities or certainties. The emphasis is on inner satisfaction. This climate can affect Christian circles. Within the Church there is a tendency to seek spirituality for the sake of one's own inner well-being. Spirituality is primarily directed towards God and others, not to self. Personal blessing comes as a by-product. Christianity was a trinitarian religion before it had a trinitarian theology. It is one thing to know the language of the doctrine of the Trinity but another to see how trinitarian truth can affect the validity of our spirituality. So, our spirituality is not to be predominantly centred on the Holy Spirit, nor exclusively centred on Christ. The Christian life is lived out in the Godhead. St Paul could say, 'Your life is hid with Christ in God'.

While recognizing the enhanced place of the emotions in charismatic worship there can be a downside. Emotions pass, when the stimulus is gone there is a tendency to flatness with resulting disappointment, batteries needing to be charged by the next experience. Dry formalism is not answered by temporary emotionalism. Mind, will and conscience are equally with emotions the field of the Holy Spirit's control.

It is not surprising that renewal of the charismatic nature can result in division among Christians. It will be particularly so when those who have experienced renewal affect a superior type of Christian experience, first-class as opposed to second-class. But, then, that is not a fault of one tradition alone. Lined up with a particular tradition out of conviction it is easy to be critical of other positions, especially within the same broad tradition. If one claims to be open evangelical, it seems to me necessary to be open not only to other evangelicals but to the other main traditions in the Church, whatever differences remain. In charity and patient debate one's own apprehension of the truth may be enriched. The diamond of God's truth has many facets.

After some 50 years in the ministry I have a much richer appreciation of the Church in God's purposes than when I began. Truly we have the treasure of the gospel in earthen vessels. I marvel at the patience and condescension of God in working with human beings so subject to failings of understanding, so prone to disagree, so guilty of confusing self-interest with loyalty to the truth. Think only of those who burned others at the stake believing they were following God's will, or of those who opposed the abolition of slavery because they thought the New Testament supported the system of slavery, or indeed of church leaders in World War One who related the killing of as may of the enemy as possible with doing God's will. I am bound to wonder what follies in today's Church test God's patience. Yet he does not abandon his Church, nor cease to use it in whatever he wills for humanity. I am forced to think again and again of God's vulnerability in creating, saving and working with human creatures. But, then, it is of the essence of love to be vulnerable to the loved one. To give men and women the freedom to respond or turn away because he loves them is to be constantly vulnerable. The theme of long-suffering loving kindness runs throughout the Bible.

And, as may well be apparent from what has gone before, I am happier to be in the Church of England today than when I began in the ministry. There have been many developments which make it a better company of Christians than when I first knew it. Of course there are new problems, new threats, and numerically the Church in the UK is weaker. But I recall that 50 years ago for many people there were much fewer counter-attractions on Sundays and inherited church-attendance habits in a less secular age were stronger. In the congregation of which I became vicar in 1954 there were two cars, one of which was really a company car. Televisions were not very numerous. Travel away from one's own neighbourhood was not very frequent. Sunday sports events were hardly known. I do not think that real commitment to seeking and following God's will was stronger then than among those who attend church now. And with a few exceptions there is greater respect and goodwill between the different traditions among clergy and laity. A bizarre illustration of former attitudes was related to me on arrival at that parish in

Bolton. The Sunday school, as was the practice, met in the afternoon. On the afternoon of Trinity Sunday the Roman Catholic parishes in Bolton held their processions around the town centre with banners and statues carried solemnly. The superintendent of our Sunday school gave strict instructions to all scholars beforehand that they were to come along the streets deliberately refusing to look at the processions. How ridiculously crazy had prejudice made him! Having arrived at Sunday school they were all to sing, 'Dare to be a Daniel, dare to stand alone!'. When I retired from that parish in 1993 I was a welcome visitor in the presbytery of the adjacent Roman Catholic parish and my wife was a fellow-chaplain with that priest in the local hospice. If these facts are evidence of greatly improved ecumenical relations the same is even more true of relationships within the Church of England. Other encouraging signs will be mentioned later. God has not forsaken the Church of England. There is hope.

# 4

# The Ministry

Looking back to the mid-twentieth century I judge there was weakness among evangelicals in their doctrines of the Church, the ministry, the sacraments. It stemmed from the mid-nineteenth century in reaction to the rising Anglo-Catholic movement. As many evangelicals reacted in a wholly negative way to the theory of evolution as promulgated by Charles Darwin so they were alarmed at the threat to their Protestant tradition from what they regarded as papist teaching. Thus they began to emphasize what the Church, the ministry, the sacraments are *not*, rather than what they are. Reference to the denigration of the visible, institutional, catholic Church has been made in the previous chapter.

The failure to engage positively in the debate for the mind of the Church of England left conservative evangelicals in a weak position. They tended to concentrate on secondary matters – what clergy wore in a service, what was on the table, standing at the north end, and so on.

Likewise the ordained ministry was not what the Catholics said it was. Anything that smacked of a priestly caste was repudiated. The priest was in no way a mediator. Private confession to a priest was a dangerous practice, even though the Prayer Book communion service allowed for confession and absolution to burdened souls. The priest had no powers to effect a valid sacrament of communion. What then was the ordained minister? A minister of the word and sacraments, primarily the former, and pastor of the flock. Essentially he was little different from the laity, because all God's people are a royal priesthood. In my early years, however, it was the negative assessment rather than the positive that still seemed to prevail. Despite their rejection of popery I knew of some vicars who acted as little popes in their parish. One, I recall, boasted of how he had got rid of awkward members of his congregation, believing he was right.

Another vicar appointed to a 'middle of the road' parish was offended by a cross and candlesticks on the altar. He sensed he would not obtain a faculty to remove them, so, as he explained, he put them in a bag and hoisted them to a high spot in the chancel so that he could claim they were still in the Church. Taking a firm line on matters at best of secondary significance was a test of 'soundness' in evangelical circles 50 years ago. The parish I came to in 1954 had had a rigid Protestant tradition in worship, weakened somewhat by a predecessor some five years earlier. He declined to wear the black gown for preaching, which entailed a visit to the vestry in the hymn before the sermon. His decision caused a big split in the congregation. On my first Sunday, as I was informed later, I was carefully watched to see if I turned east in the creed. The charge of Jesus of the religious leaders 'tything mint and cumin yet neglecting the weightier matters of the Law' seems relevant.

I believe there is still a lack of balance among evangelicals in understanding the ordained ministry. I recall a debate in General Synod on a report on this subject. Evangelical contributions to the debate were generally negative, mainly on grounds that lay ministry was not sufficiently recognized. The report seemed to me to be a positive and welcome presentation of what it was intended to be about. It was specifically about the priesthood of the ordained ministry.

A significant development for me came in 1970. In previous years there had been much attention to Anglican/Methodist reunion. A scheme to unite the two churches was opposed both by Anglo-Catholics and most evangelicals. The former said the proposed service of reconciliation failed to make Methodist ministers proper priests, the latter were against because it cast doubt on the existing ministry of the Methodists. Four theologians, two Catholic, Eric Mascall and Graham Leonard, and two evangelicals, Jim Packer and Colin Buchanan worked on an alternative scheme. They presented it in *Growing Into Union* in 1970.[20] Their proposals for a scheme of union got nowhere, but the most significant part of the book was the theological section setting out a doctrine of the Church and its ministry, including a defence of episcopacy. In the introduction the authors emphasize their complete agreement on the doctrine set out, every part. The authorship of each part was not indicated, but some years later Graham Leonard assured me that the affirmations I valued were written by Jim Packer. The key sentence I was referring to was, 'The ordained ministry is a sign of the lordship of Christ over the whole Church, including the ministers themselves'. There was more in that vein, backed by New Testament reference. The authority given by Christ is a sacramental authority, a sacrament being a sign of a spiritual entity. It must be noted that the statement does not say the ordained minister is lord over the Church in any way, but exists as a sign of Christ's lordship under which the minister serves. This seemed to me to encapsulate the authority conferred in ordination by Christ through the agency of the bishop in the historic succession of the Church catholic.

A modern trend among evangelicals seems to me to play down any difference between the ordained and the lay ministry. Emphasis on the full ministry of every member in the Body of Christ is to be welcomed and pursued, but there is a significant difference conferred by ordination. The growing habit, which I do not follow, of dispensing with robes and vestments in the leadership of main services, including communion, could be a manifestation of the desire to appear no different from the laity. It could, of course, be also a concern to appear modern, 'with it', by leaving behind inherited custom. I wonder, incidentally, whether it is what the laity want. In other areas of life official garb for those in authority is widely accepted.

Vestments are indeed a matter of secondary importance. But what is the real reason for dispensing with them even for the Eucharist? It must be intending to make a statement. We are modern, not bound to the past? We are really no different at all from the rest of the congregation? I do not accept that position.

In the debate on the priesthood of the ordained ministry previously referred to it was stressed that the following verbs sum up that priesthood, 'to enable, to represent and to signify'. I find that a more satisfactory way than conceiving of the ministry as a choice between functional terms and ontological character. 'To enable' is no problem for evangelicals. Some would cavil at 'to represent'. But in the book *Growing Into Union* it is affirmed that 'the ministry acts in the name of Christ as head of the Church'.[21] I find support for that in the Book of Common Prayer. In summoning reluctant communicants to the Lord's table the priest calls them 'in the name of God' and 'in Christ's behalf'. 'To signify' points to the ordained minister as a sign of the headship of Christ over his Church, including the ministers themselves. I believe the truth of that may be inferred from the Epistles. The idea that an ordained minister is simply a layman with a special job to do by reason of professional training is not an Anglican understanding. The Book of Common Prayer says God has given power and commandment to his ministers to declare and pronounce absolution. By God's authority committed to the minister he is to absolve the penitent sinner. I much prefer that the absolution be a declaration than turned into a prayer as some clergy do.

The ordained ministry is surely a sign in other ways than of the lordship of Christ, as the New Testament seems to say. The minister is a sign to the whole congregation of its witnessing responsibilities. He or she is not the sole witness to the gospel, but a reminder of what the whole body should be. In pastoral care the minister is a sign of the caring all should exercise. 'Be followers of me', said Paul, 'as I am of Christ.' As will be maintained later, evangelicals do not enhance the gospel by belittling the sacramental principle. The ordained ministry should not be defined solely in terms of functions. Almost all the functions, presidency of the Eucharist being an exception, can be performed by laity. The justification for ordination is not just to get someone full-time, salaried, to function, to minister all week while most of the lay leaders are working. An increasing number of clergy are in any case non-stipendiary and in secular work. The ordained person is authorized, officially commissioned by the bishop to *be* and not just to *do*. The Pastoral Epistles have material to develop this concept.

The biggest change in the ordained ministry in modern times is obviously the ordination of women. I was first challenged on my attitude in 1969. The Bishop of Manchester asked me to chair the Council for Women's Ministry. At my first meeting two ladies both strongly committed to women's ministry asked my views. I said I was in the process of working them out. At that time we had women parish workers and deaconesses. As an evangelical I had to face up to the question of headship in the Church, at that time to be exclusively male in the understanding of practically all evangelicals.

The patriarchal structure throughout Bible times, already touched on in the previous chapter, seemed to be breached in some instances in Old and New Testaments. I became convinced that the new order in God's new covenant – indicated in Galatians 3.28 – abolishing dividing barriers between male and female as well as other human orders – had eventually to be worked through. And for that, in God's providential ordering of society, modern times provided the matrix in which the full ministry of women along with men could be realized. It also seemed obvious that within the existing unordained provisions for women's ministry were persons well able and gifted to move to ordination. We could not ignore the fact, moreover, that within the missionary movement of the Church over more than a century, single women had gone overseas as missionaries. By the Lord's calling they had won converts, established churches and led them in early years. God had obviously called them and equipped them – and not just because there were not enough male missionaries.

It has to be recognized, I believe, that there are aspects of God's revelation presented in Scripture which only reach their fulfilment in the course of history. So much of the developments in the Old Testament point forward to fulfilment when the time was ripe. That was particularly true of all that pertains to the messiahship of Jesus. I do not believe the principle expired with the close of the canon. This is true to a great extent with Paul's affirmation in Galatians 3.28. A time arrives in the course of history when the impossible or the unlikely becomes possible. One cannot imagine a time before the general emancipation of women when their ordination in the Church would have been possible. Arguments against women's ordination have generally fallen under three headings. One is that Jesus never chose a woman to be among his twelve apostles. For one thing, the culture of the time would not have allowed it. And he was involved in seeking the spiritual renewal of Israel surely basing his chosen leaders on the pattern of the twelve patriarchs. For another thing, he was not concerned with the ordering of the Church and its ministry for all time. He was leaving it to the Holy Spirit to guide in the succeeding centuries. The choice of men no more determines the future of the ordained ministry than the fact that they were all Jews.

A second set of objections is focused on apostolic statements on the submission of women to men. The cultural conditioning of the first century AD has been referred to in a previous chapter. If the injunctions are to be binding in the twenty-first century, we must take them in their entirety, which even conservative Christians fail to do.

A third objection, mainly from the Catholic tradition, is that of departure from Catholic order. This amounts to little more than the Church has never done it and so the hierarchy has declared it forbidden. This touches directly on the way authority in the Church is to be exercised. In the chapter on the Church, opposition to the concept of final authority residing only in bishops has been expressed. But to suppose that in his Church as in history God will never do a new thing flies in the face of Scripture.

In one of the General Synod debates I was struck by a point made by the Bishop of Winchester, John V. Taylor. He pointed out that in God's ordering of creation humanity was called by God to act as a priesthood on behalf of all the rest of the created order in offering praise to the Creator, and to act as his representative to all the rest. And, according to Genesis 1.27, this priesthood was given to male and female as made in God's image. If through the fall this purpose was distorted, in the new creation the position is remedied. Of that new creation the Church is the sign and first-fruits. I could not foresee it at the time, 30 years ago, but the lady who is now my wife came to my parish as a parish worker, then became a deaconess, then a deacon, and after our retirement was priested. There is much personal joy in this development in the ordained ministry.

A critical position is emerging in the Church of England because of the decline in numbers of stipendiary clergy. Despite signs of an increase in ordinands, retirements and deaths more than match the intake. The situation is partly helped by the use of retired clergy. In the small deanery where my wife and I assist there are ten retired clergy, but it is one of the areas popular for retirement, not like inner-city areas. As retired clergy age their capacity to help diminishes. The only answer I can envisage is the expansion of the ordained local ministry (OLM).

Some 20 years ago I was on a working group of the Manchester and Liverpool dioceses to consider the ordination of men from inner urban, that is working-class parishes. It was believed that there were potential leaders in such churches who would not get through the normal selection procedures or cope with traditional academic training. The group presented a positive response and recommended implementation. It was agreed that their training should be *in situ*, after commendation by the PCC, and that their ministry should be confined to their home parish with, if possible, responsibility under the incumbent for some specific area of work. There would be no doubt of their ordination as priests in the Church of God. Since then the concept of OLM has expanded to include men and women from all kinds of parishes, and it has been increasingly difficult to confine their ministries to their own parish. Indeed some of the very able persons have not wanted to be so restricted and some have proceeded to stipendiary ministry.

The problem is not confined to the UK. Some years ago while on the ACC I learned of a problem in Madagascar. Not enough candidates of ability to undergo normal ordination training were to be found for all the village churches. It was decided to search out an obvious leader in these villages, give him training in his parish and ordain him. In a diocese in Kenya I was with a priest in an outlying area who was an archdeacon with 19 village congregations in his care. Services were regularly taken by a catechist or the school headteacher. The priest was only able to administer the Eucharist in each every four or five weeks. And for many communion on Easter Day was not possible. It seemed to me that the only solution was to follow the example of Madagascar. Many other areas across the Communion have the same problem, as indeed does the Roman Catholic Church.

As I will indicate later, I do not believe the answer lies in the introduction of lay presidency, as the Diocese of Sydney and some in this country want, nor in reservation of the sacrament for normal administration by the laity. A considerable increase in OLMs, operating in teams under the leadership of stipendiary priests, is surely to be encouraged and implemented as soon as possible. My wife and I assist in a team of four Anglican churches. In the team there is one OLM, who is a great asset. There should be more. Diocese after diocese is facing up to declining numbers of stipendiary clergy. The development here advocated would not be to keep every independent parish or church building going – many, especially in heavily populated dioceses should be joined to others or closed – but to provide adequate ordained support for all. Compared with much of my time in parochial ministry there are now greater pressures on the clergy, because of the financial situation, deteriorating buildings and demands of mission in an age when society is more distanced from the Church.

These pressures call for adequate pastoral care from episcopal staff. In the mid-1990s I chaired a group in the Manchester diocese charged with a review of the area system. There were three archdeaconries, each with a suffragan bishop and an archdeacon, serving under the diocesan bishop. At the time calls were being heard for a reduction of the 'chiefs' as numbers of 'Indians' declined, heard even more since then. We questioned all the senior clergy. From the diocesan bishop we learned of the very considerable demands on his time from communities across a large conurbation, in civic affairs, industry, education including university life and ecumenical relations. Although it was a unique event the aftermath of the IRA bomb in the centre of Manchester had resulted in a workload much greater than we had realized. Pastoral care of the clergy had to be largely devolved to the bishop's colleagues, whom we learned themselves were heavily committed. Our researches revealed, however, that clergy today felt a greater need of care than used to be the case. In the 39 years full time in the diocese I never received, nor expected, a visit from a bishop to my vicarage for purely pastoral reasons, though I had received them for a meal before a confirmation or other services. I knew, of course, that if I needed help or advice I could go to see any of them. In my years as an area dean I became aware of the growing vulnerability that is felt by the clergy.

One possible solution we considered was the amalgamation of the offices of area bishop and archdeacon. A suffragan bishop from a West Midlands diocese told us that when he was archdeacon his diocesan asked him to join him as a bishop. He agreed provided he could also remain archdeacon. He explained that the two roles frequently overlap in his experience. Whether that would work in an area that contains around a hundred parishes is uncertain. An example given to us of the overlap mentioned was if the archdeacon was visiting a vicarage concerning the condition of the house or the church building also discovered a relationship problem in the family requiring episcopal action. In the years since the working group reported, no action to reduce the bishop's staff has been taken, though it may become a live issue before long.

Mention of bishops and archdeacons naturally raises the question of their selection and appointment. Diocesan bishops increasingly consult within a diocese as well as with the archbishops' secretaries for appointments and the Prime Minister's secretary. Attention is directed much more strongly on the selection of diocesan bishops. For ten years I served on the Crown Appointments Commission (CAC), as it was then called, being involved in 39 appointments. In that time the methods of nomination, gathering of assessments of qualities and procedures of the Commission evolved towards more effective working. Because of the confidential nature of the deliberations mistaken impressions of that working are inevitable, some of them given credence in the media by religious correspondents. That was particularly the case in the appointment of the Archbishop of Canterbury in 1990. Sometimes, but not often, the misinformation stems from an indiscreet remark from a member of the Commission, either a permanent member or one of the diocesan representatives.

In 1987, elections to the third term of the CAC took place. The newly elected Dr Garry Bennett invited me, having already served for five years, to New College, Oxford to talk about the work of the Commission. I heard from him all the criticisms of the CAC and of Archbishop Runcie's role in it that I was later to read in his controversial Preface to Crockfords. I made it as clear as I could that on several points he was mistaken, so far as my experience of the past five years was concerned. In particular, I sought to correct his view that Archbishop Runcie dominated discussions to get his favourites selected. He also complained of the lack of appointments of strong Catholic clergy, in face of the perceived threat to that tradition from the possible ordination of women. I undertook at the first general discussion meeting of the Commission the following month to raise the matter of his concern for his tradition. He expressed satisfaction after I had done so. I also had to explain that the diocesan representatives at any meeting had uninhibited input and if convinced of the unsuitable nature of any candidate his name would not go forward. Within days of the Preface appearing there was the first meeting to consider a vacancy. For once the decision on the first of the two names to be submitted to the Prime Minister was unanimous. Afterwards Dr Bennett confessed himself satisfied with the procedure he had witnessed. In a matter of days he was dead. I am haunted by the question as to whether he sadly realized errors in the Preface written earlier in the summer. I analysed the 20 appointments made in the previous five years and found only five or so that could be described as having had any close associations with Archbishop Runcie.

The confidentiality of the system is heavily criticized. On the whole I am in favour of it. In learning of ways of appointment of bishops in other parts of the Anglican Communion I have realized how prone an open system can be to political campaigns and pressure groups, often fuelled by personal ambition. Those who advocate an open system here only seemed to see the good aspects. Candidates at present may suspect they are under consideration. There may be 12 to 15 considered for any vacancy. If one is already a diocesan bishop elsewhere it could be unsettling for him or his diocese if the news become public. Suppose someone of strong evangelical or catholic stance is widely reported as a hot tip, and is not appointed, that tradition will easily claim unfair treatment. There have been complaints recently about unfair treatment by both wings of the Church of England.

In my ten years on the Commission I never felt able to

complain about the role played by the Prime Minister. On one occasion, invited to think again about one particular diocese, we concluded there was good reason. Considerable criticism of the present system centres on the role of the Prime Minister. That role is based entirely on the establishment of the Church of England. So long as the monarch is Supreme Governor the Prime Minister must be involved as his or her advisor. When the new arrangements were agreed in 1977 it was recognized that the Prime Minister could not be merely a postman conveying the Commission's sole nomination to the Queen. That meant an element of choice should be built in, so two names would be sent forward, both of which would be deemed acceptable to the Commission.

If the Church of England were to be disestablished a new way of appointment would be necessary. But the way changes generally happen for the Church one can envisage a gradual or partial disestablishment taking place. It is anyone's guess what it would look like – perhaps a retention of the monarch's role, but freedom from the link with politics and parliament. How a nomination would be conveyed to the monarch would be a problem. It might be via the Privy Council.

I can recognize the objections to parliament having certain, though limited, powers in relation to the Church of England in the present establishment. But I still see value in other aspects of establishment. It affords various forms of access to society structures and community life which can be opportunities for service and mission. If there is value in 'keeping the rumour of God alive' we still can use those opportunities. Although occasionally one reads of some civic authority ruling out the mention of Christmas or Easter, ostensibly to avoid offence to other religions, I have never come across any determined effort to exclude Church of England participation in civic matters. If some form of establishment could enhance the partnership the Church of England has with other denominations it would be most welcome. The Christian heritage in our land may be much more fragile than in generations past but I do not believe the Church should weaken it further from our side.

My commitment to the Church of England is whole-hearted and continuing, as this chapter makes clear. But, of course, for all its members there are frustrations and irritations. What should the reaction be? It is encapsulated in a story told by Archbishop Carey when he graciously visited our parish to preach at the celebration of the fiftieth anniversary of my ordination in 2001. On a small mountain railway, as the train laboured slowly up a steep incline, some American tourists asked the driver if he couldn't go more quickly. 'Oh, yes!' he replied, 'I could go much more quickly, but I have to stay with the train!' As problems and some ensuing divisions have arisen in this congregation the story has resonated and is still referred to. Only a few day before writing this it was mentioned by one Christian lady determined 'to stay with the train'.

After ten years' experience of women in the priesthood I believe the Church of England has still a long way to go before the full benefit to their ministry and mission is realized. I am not thinking just of the full acceptance of women priests across the Church and glad acceptance across the parishes, with an eventual rescinding of the Act of Synod. The process of reception cannot go on forever. Nor am I thinking just of the opening up of the episcopate to women. It is the impact on our theology and understanding of God I am here concerned with. The starting point is the fact that in the first chapter of the Bible both male and female are made in the image of God. Whatever else is revealed by God of himself that fact can never be left behind. As already mentioned I am indebted to Bishop John V. Taylor for showing that men and women are in creation given a priestly role on behalf of all created things, to articulate the praise of them all to the Creator and to act towards them in caring role on behalf of the Creator. A subordinate role for women follows the fall, in which both sexes bear responsibility. Throughout history thereafter male dominance is seen, with just few exceptions. The Church, however, lives in the new creation inaugurated by the resurrection of Christ. It is a sign, instrument and foretaste of the kingdom of God, and as such is to exhibit the new relationships in Christ in which former divisions in human society are to be left behind. This, I believe, must mean that the original image of God is to be seen and effectively worked out in joint, harmonious partnership of men and women in the Church. As throughout biblical and church history the male reflection of God's image has predominated – and it could hardly have been otherwise – the feminine side has not had full expression. I recognize that the Bible uses male terms in speaking of God – although for the Spirit feminine nouns also appear – and Jesus himself taught us to call God Father. It could not have been otherwise. In the Old Testament, however, God is described in motherly terms. In church history theology has been done and taught by men, with just a few exceptions such as Mother Julian of Norwich, liturgy has been drawn up by men and ethical matters decided by men. Now the balance has to be carefully, painstakingly restored. Women in the full ministry are not to copy men, still less to try to do the job better than men, but to enrich the whole ministry by their God-given insights, experience and qualities. Evangelical men have as far to go in this as other traditions. Suggestions, though made in a guarded way, that women are more emotional, less able to sustain pressures, even not able to be good mothers as well as vicars, have to be recognized as male prejudices. Having observed male clergy over many years, including 20 years as an area dean I cannot be unaware of male priests' problems. As in all aspects of male personality the image of God may come through, so also is it true of female personality.

In may be helpful to review how the Anglican Communion has come to the point of considering how to deal with the issue of women bishops. While the Communion as a whole is a considerable way from agreement as to whether the consecration of women to the episcopate is in accord with God's will, there is substantial agreement on how the Communion should deal with the development. In essence the attitude to the development of women bishops has been similar to that towards women priests, with the added recognition that a woman bishop being appointed as a focus of unity could present problems in a diocese and in episcopal collegiality.

The 1968 Lambeth Conference, having affirmed that theological arguments for and against women priests are inconclusive, requested every member church to give careful study to the question and report findings to the Anglican Consultative Council, which met for the first time in 1971. Before any church finally decided to priest women the advice (the word is significant) of the ACC should be sought. The ACC having received such a request from the Council of the Church of South-East Asia on behalf of the Bishop of Hong Kong agreed by a narrow majority that the action would be acceptable to the ACC which would exercise its good offices to encourage all churches to continue in communion with the diocese concerned.

At the next meeting of the ACC in 1973, by an overwhelming majority it was agreed that ordaining women priests should not cause any break in communion in the Anglican family, and that while ecumenical repercussions should be taken into account, they should not be decisive (54 in favour, 1 against). It is recognized here that any church tradition in the worldwide fellowship of churches has authority to do whatever it is convinced the universal Church should do, after consultation, without being held-up interminably.

The Lambeth Conference in a full, detailed resolution confirmed the attitude taken at the ACC with the strong recommendation to preserve communion. The voting was 317 to 36. The Conference went on to discuss the consecration of women to the episcopate and recommended that no decision should be taken to do so 'without consultation with the episcopate through the primates and overwhelming support in any member church and the diocese concerned'. Clearly the introduction of women into the priesthood and possibly the episcopate profoundly affected the unity of the Anglican Communion and in particular its exercise of authority.

At the 1978 Lambeth Conference a 'Primates' Committee', set up to help the Archbishop of Canterbury and advise him, led the Conference to agree to support subsequent meetings of the primates, though their purpose was not wholly clear. In the early years of the Primates' Meeting its part in Communion affairs was undefined. At its 1979 meeting the minutes indicate that decisions which have legal authority are made by the synods of the provinces. The Primates' Meeting could not be, and was not desired as, a higher synod. It was a clearing house for ideas and experiences through free expression, the fruits of which they might convey to their churches.

As happens with committees, the Primates' Meeting came to define its role more clearly, and meet more frequently. Primates, as with bishops generally, are not necessarily theologians for exploration of divisive issues. It was a wise step, therefore, for them to set up a commission, chaired by Archbishop Eames, which produced the report 'Unity and Diversity Within the Communion: A way forward'. More frequent meetings and enhancement of the role of the Primates'

Meeting has tended to overshadow the role of the ACC, which, mainly for financial reasons, cannot meet more frequently than once every three years.

The Eames report described the way authority is experienced at Communion level as a power of persuasion exercised through four instruments: the Lambeth Conference, the Primates' Meeting, the ACC, together with the Archbishop of Canterbury. The long-standing rejection of any central, juridical governing body, overriding the autonomy of member churches, was maintained, as it has been ever since. As a result of reaction from the ACC in 1987 the report was amended to emphasize that

> the authority of a bishop is twofold; that which is inherent in the office of a bishop (acting in the apostolic tradition as a personal sign of the Church's continuity and unity and on behalf of the people of God within the body of Christ) and that which is expressed by the bishop in council.

Member churches were asked to react to the report, and a paper presented to the 1988 Lambeth Conference, entitled 'Instruments of Communion and Decision-Making' received widespread support.

At the 1988 Lambeth Conference, with the Episcopal Church of the United States of America (ECUSA) likely to appoint a woman bishop, it was resolved 'That each Province respect the decision and attitudes of other Provinces in the ordination or consecration of women in the episcopate, without such respect indicating acceptance of the principles involved, maintaining the highest possible degree of communion with the Provinces that differ'. Recognizing the hurt that could be caused on both sides, pastoral provision should be required (423 in favour, 28 against, 19 abstentions). It was also decided that the Archbishop of Canterbury, in consultation with the other primates, set up a commission to help process of reception and offer guidelines.

A commission chaired by Archbishop Eames on 'Communion and Women in the Episcopate' was set up which took up study previously done by a working party led by Archbishop Grindrod of Australia. The commission's guidelines offered ways of maintaining the highest degree of communion possible in the face of doctrinal disagreement and diversity of practice. Consequent upon the appointment of the first woman bishop in ECUSA the provision of episcopal visitor for congregations objecting to women bishops was suggested. It is worth noting the emphasis in the 1988 resolution on maintaining the highest possible degree of communion, and in contrast the unilateral attitude of ECUSA in the consecration of Gene Robinson, already warned of the consequences for unity in the Communion.

The Commission's report was approved at the 1998 Lambeth Conference, recognizing the ongoing, open process of reception in the Communion. Further reflection on the meaning and nature of communion was undertaken at a meeting of church leaders and theologians at Virginia Seminary in the USA. Its title was 'Belonging Together'. That report too was endorsed at Lambeth 1998. More recently, a further commission led by Archbishop Eames has produced the Windsor Report. Though the context is different from women in the episcopate, being occasioned by the even more divisive issue of reaction to homosexual practices, particularly involving clergy and bishops, the concern for the highest degree of communion is carried forward.

In the latter part of the year 2005 the Synod of the Church of Nigeria took a decision which if carried through, and possibly copied by others, would change the nature and basis of communion in Anglicanism. It appears to be based on a belief that the Anglican Church is a confessional church, the

39 Articles being cited. It has been strongly maintained earlier that neither the Articles nor the Lambeth Quadrilateral is a confession in the sense that obtained in other churches of the Reformation. Nor could any member church's own definition of 'the apostolic faith' be the essential basis of what it means to be in communion, still less of one church's interpretation of Scripture. If a tradition in the Church is strong and long-established it can easily fall into the error of believing that only those who agree with its detailed understanding of the faith are to be regarded as in communion. As I have earlier indicated this was the attitude of conservative evangelicals 70 years ago. It ought not to be so now.

In my 15 years on the Anglican Consultative Council I came to a deep appreciation of the Anglican Communion, not least in churches now known as the global South. Their commitment to evangelism is both an example and a challenge to older churches. And older churches need the Communion. It seems it would be a tragic folly for the Communion to be split over an issue of the interpretation of small sections of Scripture in seeking the will of God for our own day. We need to stay together, praying, talking, open to the Holy Spirit.

# 5

# The Sacraments

When I was baptized at a few weeks old my father asked the vicar using the 1662 baptism service to omit after the baptismal act the words 'Seeing now that this child is regenerate'. Telling me this years later it was clear that he could not accept the positive nature of sacramental language. To him the service was essentially the dedication of an infant to God. He was no doubt typical of very many evangelical parents, and probably clergy, of the time. I do not regard myself as having been deprived of the blessings of the sacrament, though I later came to a different approach from my father.

At Keele 1967 the Congress in the section 'The Church and its worship' declared: 'In view of the widespread misunderstanding caused by such expressions as "this child is regenerate", we would welcome . . . revision, provided that the covenant basis which they express is not lost.' There is no doubt about the scriptural foundation of infant baptism but strong condemnation of indiscriminate baptism as a scandal demanding remedy. Its practice is seen as productive of the current divisive reaction against infant baptism.

In the 1960s I was asked to prepare two small booklets on Baptism and the Lord's Supper for translation in the Burmese languages in the mission stations of the Bible Churchmen's Missionary Society. This occasioned a clarification of my theology of the sacraments.

I concluded that the categorical language at the heart of the rites of baptism and holy communion could not be weakened by provisional, conditional clauses. The place for emphasizing the conditions for worthy, that is, effective reception of the sacrament was in foregoing parts of the service. Repentance and faith had to be clear and stressed, but the declaration accompanying the administration had to be definite. Recipients who were responding to God sincerely must be in no doubt as to his saving love. In fact, in revisions of the baptism services while the regenerate phrase has not been repeated as such, there is clear, unambiguous declaration of the benefit of the sacrament. The efficacy of the sacraments depends on the institution and command of Christ. Statements in the New Testament on their efficacy are unequivocally clear, though the right human response is similarly clear.

As for the scandal of indiscriminate child baptism deplored at Keele, continuing division has focused on baptismal discipline in parishes. Some exercise a tight discipline, requiring a period of church attendance, whatever reactions from families. I came to regard this approach as less effective than its supporters supposed. Whatever hoops parents are required to get through there can be no guarantee they will come to faith. Sacramental discipline is not primarily directed to easing the minister's conscience. There is a parallel with parents clocking in for a year or so at church in order to get their child into a church school. They are subject to hearing the gospel for a time and to pastoral care but in the end their motivation is paramount. Are they going through the motions or genuinely open to God?

Mention has already been made of the times of apostasy in Israel. The sacrament of circumcision was not withheld or temple worship ordered to be suspended, but true prophets of the Lord addressed the sins of the people. Every care must be taken, I believe, in sensitive preparation of baptism families, and follow-up procedures, but in the end we can only accept professed declarations of response. To repeat the old adage, 'we cannot make windows into men's souls'.

Thus, baptism is a firm pledge and affirmation of God's saving purposes towards the person concerned. All the blessings of salvation are personally pledged, whatever the age of the recipient. The prayer of the minister, the congregation, and, it is hoped, the family, is that those blessings will be steadily appropriated by repentance and faith throughout life. Despite my father's misgivings about the words used over me, within five and a half years with the prayerful help of my parents I took the first conscious step I can remember of trusting in Jesus Christ. It was a result of something I heard at a beach mission in Eastbourne on holiday. I have no doubt in the closing years of my life I have still to enter into more of the blessings pledged in my baptism.

All Christians, I believe, need to find assurance of salvation. Those of a Catholic tradition find it mainly in reception of the sacraments. That is why they need to be sure of the validity of a sacrament. Evangelicals look to the word of the gospel. I have come to hold to both word and sacrament. Through what both pledge the inner assurance of the Spirit is given. So as well as rejoicing in what the word conveys I am enriched in assurance to say, I am baptized. Baptism, however, is not just a sacrament of assurance. As Paul particularly emphasizes in his letters it is a constant challenge to realize in daily living the fact of being incorporated into the death and resurrection of Christ. Be holy not just because the word of God says so, but because you are baptized.

This is clearly articulated in the long exhortation at the end of the baptism service in the Book of Common Prayer. While the service is perhaps too wordy for modern ears I am not entirely happy with the current modern services. They cram in a plethora of theological or doctrinal themes, all of them biblical and expressive of the meaning of baptism. For the families already in the Church that is acceptable. In our small town, however, most baptisms are for families with little or no regular connection. Crowds of families and friends turn up, generally for a post-morning service administration. Because of the number of baptisms it is normally those of church members that are taken in the main service. No doubt the party arranged after is a draw for some of the large numbers entering hesitantly as regular worshippers leave for home. This, unlike most inner urban areas, is an area where folk look to the Church for baptisms and weddings. It would be unrealistic to regard these occasions as great evangelistic opportunities, but impressions are created, for good or ill. If most of those present at a baptism find the language of the service incomprehensible an opportunity for building bridges could be lost. A good impression can be made by the welcome given, the short address by the priest, and his or her kindness. I wonder, therefore, if a form of service concentrating on the main point of baptism could be available, used at the discretion of the administrant.

## Holy communion

Celebration of the holy communion was low in the priorities of evangelical worship 60 years ago, but so it was in most parishes. There could be an 8 o'clock celebration for a small number who turned up, but the main services were morning prayer and evening prayer. After ordination it was a welcome experience to have a monthly service entirely of holy communion. Moving to my parish in Bolton the pattern I inherited was morning prayer followed by a shortened communion for those who chose to stay – 'mangled mattins'

– with a similar arrangement in the evening, on alternate Sundays. In my first year I was faced with an annual event which was really a Sunday school anniversary and gift day in one. The pattern was a 9 a.m. prayer meeting, a procession of witness at 9.30 a.m. (largely through empty streets), morning prayer at 10.30 a.m., afternoon service for the Sunday schools and Bible classes, concluding with evening prayer. A visiting preacher was a must. I tentatively asked if there was no communion service, and was told there was no time for one on that special day. After a year or two I suggested to the PCC that once a month we should have a communion as a main service. There was some resistance. One man said the Prayer Book only required reception of communion three times a year. The change, however, was agreed 'as an experiment', provided that there was opportunity for folk to leave if they wished before the administration. The experiment eventually, after many years, became a weekly event at the main service.

The Keele Congress statement in 1967 makes the following admission:

> We have failed to do justice in our practice to the twin truths that the Lord's Supper is the main service of the people of God and that the local church, as such is the unit within which it is properly administered . . . we have let the sacrament be pushed to the outer fringes of church life, and the ministry of the Word be divorced from it . . . We determine to work towards the practice of a weekly celebration of the sacrament as the central corporate service of the church.

Now that the aim in that statement has been mainly achieved in almost all evangelical churches some problems remain. With the decline in Sunday schools all-age worship services have come in as a main service in many parishes, with the hope of attracting unattached parents and friends. The problem of such 'visitors' getting further in commitment is recognized. Perhaps there is undue recognition that the sacrament can be 'a converting ordinance'. If effort is made to assure non-communicants there is no shame in not receiving, or encouraging them to come up for a blessing prayer, a desire for greater commitment could be encouraged.

The Lord's Supper is not just an occasion for individuals to receive the means of grace. It is essentially the place and the way the local church identifies itself and is identified. In the celebration the company of believers is seen as the Body of Christ in that place. 'We being many are one Body.' As in no other activity of a Christian congregation the members demonstrate by action – partaking at the Lord's Table – their unity with one another in Christ. They also by their participation witness to the culmination of God's saving purposes in heaven, the marriage supper of the Lamb. They share in this earthly eucharistic meal 'till He comes'.

As reflection on baptism and its significance can add to the word in establishing assurance of God's acceptance of the believer, so receiving holy communion in faith confirms that acceptance. Every believer should come away from the communion rail with renewed assurance of being fully saved by grace. That is one reason why I prefer the ending of modern forms of the Eucharist over the 1662 service. In the latter the Gloria just before the Benediction has repetitive requests for mercy. Individually all may before leaving church express penitence for imperfections in their worship. But the predominant expression should be of confident thanksgiving. The Gloria is well placed at an earlier point in the Eucharist.

With this view of the sacrament I believe the right president of the Eucharist is the ordained minister. It is not that a lay leader could not perform the action of presiding. It is that, if the ordained minister is a sign of the lordship of Christ over the Church, as has been maintained, that sign should be evident when the local church is identified as the Body of Christ. His or her presidency in the Eucharist is surely required. With the ordained minister's authority goes the ultimate authority for exercise of discipline in the Church. While its exercise may very seldom be necessary there can be occasions when administration has to be withheld from individuals. I have only once in my ministry suggested to the churchwardens they should discourage an individual from receiving communion. Whether I was right I have to leave to God's judgement.

## Confirmation

It was long regarded in the Anglican Church that confirmation by a bishop was the essential gateway to communion. Confirmation has all through that time been a rite with no agreed theology. For many Catholics, and others searching for meaning, it was the rite for receiving the Holy Spirit. For evangelicals generally it was the occasion for checking the readiness of candidates for communion by reason of repentance and faith. There is now increasing recognition that baptism is in itself the full rite of initiation into the Body of Christ. In baptism the Holy Spirit is fully pledged. And though confirmation is an opportunity for instruction in the faith, teaching on the Lord's Supper and commitment in discipleship as the candidate makes a public affirmation of vows made by proxy or personally in baptism, it adds nothing vital to baptism. As a consequence of this understanding many evangelicals are prepared to admit children to communion before confirmation when they are perceived to be capable of a simple understanding of the Lord's Supper. Confirmation is then deferred to a more mature age when the implications of life-long discipleship can be more surely grasped. It has long been apparent that confirmees between childhood and puberty were more taken up with the occasion than its significance. It is little wonder confirmation turned out to be in effect 'a leaving ceremony'.

Those with doubts about this development have questioned whether children can worthily receive the sacrament. Experience convinces me they can. I am conscious also that the equivalent sacrament in the old covenant, the Passover, was attended by the whole family with the youngest playing a part. Should the sacrament of a new and better covenant be more restricted in its scope and benefit?

The Church of England has struggled to find agreement on the meaning and administration of confirmation for decades. In the first quinquennium of General Synod a report on Christian initiation was debated – it was not the first report. I was required to chair a small working group to prepare for the debate on the report. As I expected in presenting our suggestions the reaction was very mixed. Since then progress has been made. And, if I may say, bishops' addresses at confirmation have improved since I first went round as an area dean attending them. Over recent years I have not heard bishops telling bemused candidates, 'You are about to receive the Holy Spirit'. The laying on of hands is, of course, a biblical practice signifying a prayer of blessing or commissioning. In confirmation it is both.

We do no service to biblical truth by belittling the sacramental principle in God's economy. The rainbow, circumcision, the Passover, the sacrificial system in the Old Testament, baptism, the Lord's Supper, the laying on of hands in the New Testament are all instances of visible signs signifying spiritual truths. Matter and spirit are linked in God's dealings with humanity. We must avoid the ancient philosophical concept of matter as evil and spirit alone to be confirmed. The Christian faith is of all religions uniquely incarnational, even though there have been times under the influence of Greek philosophical concepts when the significance of matter has been underestimated.

Evangelicals have generally tended to prioritize the ministry of the word over the sacraments. They have emphasized that the word preached makes clear the way of God in saving and sanctifying his people, whereas it is possible for recipients of the sacraments to have a superstitious and ill-instructed attitude to them. In this attitude there may be failure to recognize that the ministry of the word is subject to human fallibility, inadequate grasp of biblical truth and less than pure motivation. God may still use a sermon to convey his grace. In the sacraments, if administered according to Christ's words of institution and with the elements prescribed, the offer of grace is guaranteed to all who believe. There need be no imbalance of between word and sacrament. Lest it be thought I cast doubt on the preaching of the word, I have, since I was first asked to preach in a mission hall at the age of 15, regarded preaching as an enormous privilege and responsibility. As someone has said, it is a royal sacrament. But throughout the years I have been very conscious of the preacher's temptation in motivation. Because I enjoy it, personal fulfilment and desire for approbation have to be suppressed, and the glory of God and the blessing of the people supreme.

# 6

# Worship and Liturgy

In the present day worship in evangelical churches has moved from an earlier total commitment to the Book of Common Prayer to a diversity influenced by Series 2 and 3, the ASB, Common Worship, all-age worship, and the Charismatic Movement. A minority of church people deplore the departure from the 1662 book and condemn modern forms as banal and shallow, the language failing to induce reverence. While I am happy to celebrate with the 1662 communion in one of the four churches in the team ministry my wife and I help in, I do not criticize the language or structures or content of current liturgy. There is a lack of reverence in worship in many evangelical churches, but not due to language change. Sense of the holiness of God seems to be absent. A 'matey' approach towards God and fellow worshippers is preferred, possibly stimulated by some modern songs and style of leadership of the service. People are used to the style of MCs on TV chat-shows, but I believe ministers in worship should shun anything approaching that style. Indeed, I wonder whether a congregation needs to be told what it is going to do next – 'we are now going to confess our sins' – when they have the book in their hands. A particular concern since having occasion to be in the congregation rather than leading is the lack of reverence during the administration of communion. Widespread conversations on a variety of topics begin before or after receiving. I imagine a lot of folk didn't know how to use the time profitably. I regret that in active parochial ministry I did not give more attention to help worshippers in this matter, and indeed in knowing how to meditate. A simple framework can be four 'looks' – a look back to give thanks for a full atonement made at Calvary, a look up to receive afresh from the ascended Lord his life of purity, power and purpose, a look around to recognize the corporate communion with God's people, a look ahead to the marriage supper of the Lamb.

One positive feature of modern forms of the Eucharist is the wider range of biblical truth than in the 1662 service. The latter was intended to be with morning prayer but taken in isolation focuses exclusively on the cross; there is a paucity of reference to other truths.

A set liturgy will involve ritual. It is a mark of evangelical worship to keep ritual simple. It is even more important that it should signify true doctrine and assist a spirit of reverence. I am prepared to accommodate myself generally to customs in serving in another church. Turning to the east in the creed is not a problem, even if those concerned don't know the origin of the custom. Other bits of Catholic ritual seem to me of doubtful value. Carrying the Bible with accompanying candles into the nave for the reading of the Gospel is one example. The Gospels do contain the words of Jesus but the Epistles are equally inspired by God as unfolding the truths of Christ's saving actions in the cross and resurrection. Of course, we all stand for the Gospel, even in the most Protestant of churches! All ritual should serve to illustrate the truth of the Gospel and its expression in worship.

A new provision in modern services of baptism is the conferring of a lighted candle. It can make a good point. One very helpful ritual matter I learned from a Catholic friend on the liturgical committee of the Synod, Donald Gray. It was at the time of the launching of Series 2 communion. It was a mistake, he said, for the celebrant to wave his hands about ostentatiously in the thanksgiving prayer. The consecration of the elements was not done by the priest, still less by his actions. Consecration was by the thanksgiving of the whole congregation articulated by the priest in the required words. I would add that any ritual fussily drawing attention to the minister is inappropriate, as is also undue attention by the minister to his leadership by his interventions. A set liturgy needs sensitive, clear, audible, but also unobtrusive leadership. In the pulpit preaching is truth through personality, to quote a famous American preacher of former days. Preaching reflects the preacher's grasp of the truth in the exposition of Scripture. In liturgy the leader can be anonymous as far as possible.

Robes or vestments for a long time signified churchmanship divisions. Well into the second half of the twentieth century a few churches insisted on the black gown for preaching. In the hymn before the sermon the preacher would have to retire to the vestry to change from surplice to gown. It was supposed to stress the ministry of the word. For all other activities surplice, scarf and hood were obligatory in evangelical churches. Ordinands were encouraged to resist wearing a white stole at ordination, as stoles and accompanying vestments were regarded as signifying a sacerdotal concept of priesthood. With my vicar's encouragement in Durham I borrowed a white stole for my ordination as the bishop attached no doctrinal significance to it. When canon law was revised the canon dealing with vestments clearly affirmed that bishop's judgement. As a consequence many evangelical clergy have no problems in departing from scarf and hood for eucharistic services and following liturgical colours according to the season. What was once thought to be of primary importance for evangelicals is now relegated to a secondary concern. This is just one example of the way a sense of priorities for evangelicals has evolved.

Another major mark of identification was 'north end' at communion. The fact that for some time after the sixteenth century the position of the table was not against the east wall did not diminish the importance of taking a stance different from the eastward position. When the westward position began to be adopted there was some alarm in evangelical circles. A booklet was hastily prepared by three leading churchmen resisting the westward position. It became an issue one year at the Southport Evangelical Conference. Colin Buchanan, then establishing himself as a liturgiologist, exposed the booklet's deficiencies. I was convinced by him. If, as had been suggested, the spot behind the table should be for the Lord, though invisible, and the minister as his servant should be at the north end, the consequences were quite remarkable. If we believe the Lord was located there, an appropriate response was to bow towards him! The Lord is not absent in the Eucharist, but is present by his Spirit in all his people present: 'The Lord is here, his Spirit is with us.' The westward position is the most natural and convenient place for the president to be. It enables the taking and the breaking to be most clearly seen, as they should be.

With the Eucharist now the main, and for most worshippers the only act of worship on a Sunday, there is value in some flexibility in its form and contents. While some Christians, notably of the older generation, want everything to be as in the past with strict adherence to a well-loved pattern many more welcome variations, now provided in Common Worship forms. Fifty years ago, as I recall, some elderly ladies in my congregation expressing deep appreciation of one of my predecessors, said, 'he was a great preacher, though we did not really understand what he was saying'. They were jut happy to be there doing the familiar things. With increased educational standards attitudes are different. Furthermore, due to modern presentations in the media and TV programmes folk are conditioned to swift flowing movement and different themes. Their attention span is shorter. When I started preaching, a sermon in the region of 25 minutes was expected. A service seldom lasted less than an hour and a quarter. Over the years I cut down sermons to around 15 minutes, and some have said that was too long! With the decline of the Sunday school movement and growth of all-age worship the flexibility now available is very welcome. As long as there is ministry of the word and the words of institution by Christ in the thanksgiving, with the elements prescribed, the intention of the Eucharist is safeguarded. And children can gain benefit from the sacrament in modern form.

# 7

# Mission

Many of my relatives and friends of an older generation had come to faith through evangelistic campaigns such as those by Fritz (later Fred) and Arthur Wood of the Young Life Campaign. Fred was the preacher, his brother was in charge of the music. Their campaigns covered the early decades of the twentieth century. A very early memory I have is of being propelled across the stage of a theatre in Preston to present a bouquet to La Marechale, an evangelist associated with the Booth family of Salvation Army fame. So I was predisposed to enthusiastic support of evangelism by campaigns, missions, or crusades, as they later came to be called. Hence I became heavily involved in rallies from the Billy Graham Crusade in 1954 and in the next year from Glasgow. In 1961 I was on the committee for the North of England Crusade by Billy Graham in Manchester, and tried to get my parish fully involved. A visitation of the parish five times in the preceding months to invite anyone to accompany us without charge to the rallies was diligently undertaken. I have no doubt that many across the region were brought to personal faith, but the impact on my parish in all these events, and a similar local town crusade, was very limited.

Reflection on these concentrated efforts led me to believe that after initial curiosity by unchurched members of the public in the Harringay Crusade in 1954, interest was not sufficient to persuade them to travel some 15 miles to repeat crusades. As one who had for some of these crusades a responsibility in dealing with the cards completed by counsellors after helping enquirers who had responded to the invitation to 'come forward', I began to question the effectiveness of the concept of a brief contact between strangers allegedly leading to a profession of faith. I do not question the effectiveness in some cases. But there seemed to be the assumption in the training course that a set pattern of counselling could deal with all enquirers. For some, at any rate, the reasons for coming forward were deep and complicated. As a result the attempt to link up enquirers with churches failed in many cases, perhaps sometimes the fault of the church to which referral was made. I increasingly believe the path to a living and lasting relationship with Christ is for many long and gradually pursued, and that the role of Christian friends cannot be exaggerated.

Evangelism in the context of large rallies with massed choirs had begun in the USA in the nineteenth century. The most prominent of the evangelists was D. L. Moody, his music assistant was Sankey. They also came to Britain. In a day when sources of entertainment were much less accessible the rallies attracted large crowds. Ordinary folk were also less inclined to critical questioning of those who spoke with authority. This is not to deny that many came to faith who were not otherwise reached by established churches. The vast crowds who flocked to hear Billy Graham later in the twentieth century testify to the continuing effect of this form of evangelism. Alongside these campaigns by prominent evangelists arose movements like Youth for Christ, Campus Crusade, Operation Mobilisation. In the twenty-first century in Britain, at any rate, with its postmodern, secular culture evangelism demands a different approach with local churches acting much more along the lines of relationships within the local community.

I am grateful for the suggestion in the former Bishop of Liverpool David Sheppard's autobiography that 'stepping stones' are needed for non-churchgoers to begin to relate to the Christian community. It has been customary to talk of 'bridges' to enable that journey. A bridge suggests one structure easily crossed. Stepping stones involve several contact points less easy to cross and often needing a helping hand. The evangelistic task today requires a local congregation to explore stepping stones.

A most welcome development in mission has been the recognition of its relevance and meaning across churchmanship divisions. In 1954 in a large deanery chapter an evangelical incumbent of another parish from my own suggested to the clergy that in the light of the Billy Graham Crusade we have a debate about mission. The response of a number of the clergy was that it was not necessary. Mission was what happened in countries overseas, not in England. It is not a response one would hear today.

Various national initiatives in evangelism were attempted in the 1970s. There was a Call to the North. Then a National (later changed to Nationwide) Initiative in Evangelism (NIE) was launched when Archbishop Coggan was at Canterbury. It was an ambitious concept, drawing together the British Council of Churches, representatives of the main churches, and the more independent evangelical bodies. I was not the only one on the committee to find it frustrating despite evident enthusiasm for reaching out to the nation. Some were very wary of the possibility of a crusade type of approach, whereas others were in favour. And it became apparent that no agreement on the presentation of the gospel between the more independent evangelicals and others was possible. By the 1980s the NIE folded. The title of a report on its work was 'The Unwanted Child'.

Much reflection on the Decade of Evangelism has taken

place, not always with accuracy, particularly in the media. It was not initiated in England by Archbishop George Carey. It was the Lambeth Conference in 1988 – three years before George Carey became Archbishop – where the idea of a decade at the end of the twentieth century of concentrated evangelism was advocated by bishops from the developing world. To their credit many of the bishops pursued the idea energetically. Nigeria, for instance, appointed nine men to be missionary bishops to go and evangelize and establish new dioceses. In England the ethos of society was much more resistant to evangelism. But at least there was increasing desire in many churches to see growth, to be more effective in evangelism, even if this was accompanied by puzzlement as to how it could happen. We ought, but we don't know how to, was the general feeling. However some helpful initiatives were taken, the Springboard for Evangelism in which Archbishop Carey took the initiative, and mission directors in dioceses, among them. Those initiatives continue to bear fruit in many parishes, even though evangelism in our post-Christian society is far harder than in some parts of the world, where the Church is growing at a fast rate.

So far mission in this chapter has been taken to equal evangelism. In the 1970s evangelicals became more aware that mission was a wider concept than bringing people to faith in Christ. It also meant practical care for the needy, alleviation of poverty, working for just structures in society. More extreme liberals were accusing evangelicals engaged in acts of mercy of using them to bribe converts. On the Board for Mission and Unity of General Synod a draft report on mission was heavily criticized for lack of balance. A subsequent working group I chaired attempted to give evangelism its full place within the broader understanding of mission, which in fact comprises all the Church is sent into the world to do for God's kingdom. In the Anglican Communion the

ACC drew up a four-point definition of mission incorporating these principles, later adding a fifth point relating to environmental concerns, as has already been noted.

In retirement I have concluded that issues of social justice have not featured as strongly in my concept of mission as they ought, despite the fact that I supported their inclusion in a Board of Mission document in the 1970s. On reflection I realize my mind had earlier been conditioned by evangelical aversion to a social gospel as being a denial of the vital work of bringing people to faith in Christ.

Up to World War Two in addition to membership of my parish church I was also involved with its mission hall in a slum area of the parish where my father acted as superintendent. The poverty and deplorable housing conditions all around were all too evident. The small mission hall community, all from outside the immediate area, had no power to remedy the situation. Their only response, as they saw it, was by open-air meetings, tract distribution and invitation to services to try to bring individuals to conversion.

In more recent times exposure on television of the appalling conditions across the world in which millions of fellow human beings have to exist has brought home their plight to more affluent peoples. Responses to ad hoc appeals for financial help have grown in volume. But radical, and costly, remedies have been very slow to emerge. The Church's mission has to be as firmly committed to social justice as to the salvation of souls. It is impossible to read the writings of the prophets of the Old Testament without recognizing the demands of Jehovah in social matters. The ministry of Jesus in no way lessened those demands. And the Church as a sign, instrument and foretaste of the kingdom of God fails in its mission if it neglects them.

I have recently been struck in reading the autobiography of David Sheppard by the way his whole thinking was formed on social justice. From a public school background, inter-national fame as a cricketer and evangelical conversion, he became immersed in the Mayflower Centre in the East End of London. There, and in his experience in Liverpool, working for justice to the deprived became a burning passion of his life. So committed was he to that cause that he declined a move to the more congenial sphere at Oxford. The cost of the Church's involvement in a campaign for social justice is to be labelled by others as Marxist. But we follow a Master who was constantly criticized by those with vested interests.

# 8

# Eschatology

Before and up to World War Two an evangelical body called the Advent Testimony and Preparation Movement existed. Taking the apocalyptic passages in the Old and New Testament quite literally as God's programme for the next few years the speakers proved fascinating to me as a teenager. Jesus was returning very soon, would return to the Mount of Olives, there would be an almighty battle at Armageddon; the Church would be caught up, the dead resurrected from their graves to join those alive at the time and Christ would then reign on earth for a thousand years. Much detail of how nations, at least in Europe, would line up was confidently given. It was not the first time, nor will it be the last, that the parousia was said to be almost immediate.

During my student days I took part in a mission in the Potteries, involving Anglican parishes. I learned, however, that at the time there were around 40 Brethren Assemblies, due to splits from other assemblies of the same tradition over interpretation of biblical prophesies, often in relation to minor detail. No doubt they were all contending for the truth of Scripture.

Bible study soon led me to a different way of understanding the apocalyptic genre in Scripture. What do I now believe? That the parousia of Christ is as certain as the resurrection, that God will complete his purposes through Christ of a consummation in new heavens and earth, that through the resurrection God's people will know their redeemed and perfected spirits united with a body fit for heaven. But what of those not among the redeemed? I do not follow the universalist line that in the end every human being will be saved, even if there are some verses in the New Testament that might be interpreted to that end. Human beings have been given the capacity to say NO to God, to reject his salvation. What is their destiny? Undoubtedly heaven and hell are both presented in Scripture. If heaven is being with God, hell is being separated from God. The large question here concerns immortality. Is immortality, existence for ever and ever, a reality inherent in being human? The question is complicated by our inability to understand the meaning of eternity. We tend to think of it as unending time, but time itself is part of the present created order. I question whether every human being possesses immortality. Through the Fall and our participation in its consequences we are dead towards God, separated. But Scripture tells us we can receive the gift of eternal life through faith in Christ. We are thus born again, made partakers of the divine nature. 'The wages of sin is death [spiritual separation from God], the gift of God is eternal life through Jesus Christ our Lord' (Rom. 6.23). This inclines me to regard immortality of the spirit as conditional upon that gift in grace through faith. There is much in the New Testament not covered in the foregoing thoughts. Interpretation of the language, much of it in pictorial form, will continue to be argued over. In heaven I expect to learn where I have been right and where wrong

I have been much helped by Jürgen Moltmann's *Theology of Hope*.[22] The God we worship is the God of hope. The tendency of believers is to think of God in terms of the past and the present, if I am not mistaken. He is the Creator of the universe some 14 billion years ago. He called out a people to whom he revealed his will and purposes. He became incarnate in Jesus 2000 years ago, who died and rose again in the Holy Land. We inherit a Church from past history. And now in our lifetime we know God's present grace, indwelling and guidance. If asked what God means to us we tend to express it in terms of past and present. But throughout biblical history God is revealed as looking to the future. After the fall of humanity a future Saviour was promised. Abraham, living in a settled, civilized community, is told to get out for a still unknown land, where he will become the father of a future people of God. In slavery in Egypt the people are led out by Moses to the Promised Land. When through their sinful rebellion they are taken into exile, God sends his prophets to promise a return. And in various ways through the history a coming Messiah is promised. A consistent inclination of God's people is to remain in their present condition, or even when in desert wanderings to return to their past.

With Jesus, however, came the resurrection, and that is much more than a guarantee of his continuing living presence, or even a pledge of future bliss for the individual believer. The resurrection inaugurated and established the pattern of God's New Creation to be consummated in the parousia of Christ. In the resurrection appearances both continuity with the past and discontinuity are seen. Although not immediately recognizable he reveals himself to be the same person in a way and at a time he chooses. But he has the same relationships, evokes the same trust, demonstrates the same love. He still calls his own sheep by name. There is, however, discontinuity. No pain, no bodily decay, no bodily functions – the action of eating is surely in order to convince that he was not a disembodied spirit. What has this to say about the new heavens and earth? There must be discontinuity with all that has been temporary, subject to suffering, decay, death, but continuity with all that is essentially good we have known.

I do not think we can assume from the resurrection appearances that the resurrection body we will be given will have likeness to our present bodies, with head, torso, arms and legs. Unless Jesus had appeared in that form his risen life would not have been recognized. Our present bodies are what they are because of the way with the animal kingdom we have evolved. All we can say is that without a body of some kind we will not be human in eternity. It will be as St Paul says, a spiritual body perfectly suited to our redeemed spirits. One has only to ask the question, at what age of our earthly existence we would want the resurrected body to liken, to realize its changed nature. The infant, the child, the disabled person, the elderly struggling with bodily weakness will find a different existence.

# 9

# Culture and Moral Problems

In the Introduction I described briefly the concept of worldliness in evangelical churches at the time of my upbringing. The list of those pursuits forbidden to Christians was lengthy. One problem with living within that kind of list of taboos is that some will want to indulge in one or other of the items, but will have to do it secretly. I know of individuals looking up and down the street before creeping into a cinema, or having a cigarette in secret. The fact is Christians of that age and tradition had not worked out their relationship to culture.

Christ and culture is a constant challenge to the Church, demanding changing responses as ages come and go. There is always much that Christ challenges in contemporary culture, other matters he can affirm and others of neutral value on which individual Christians can make up their minds as they establish their priorities.

Joining the Navy at 18, straight from school, I was catapulted into a vastly different environment. I certainly did not throw overboard all the ideas I had inherited. Indeed, aversion to much I witnessed led to some appreciation of the lifestyle of parents and relations. But questions began to arise.

In my curacy in Durham an incident occurred which afterwards forced more thorough reflection. I was in charge of the youth club. It was suggested that we have a barn dance, an idea of which the vicar, John Wenham, approved. Still inhibited by my early upbringing I said I could not go through with it. Indeed, if it went ahead I might feel obliged to move to another parish. Later reflection led me to realize that anxiety of what my parents would say underlay my attitude. I knew it upset John, more than I realized at the time, because in his autobiography, he singles it out from my time there. I believe there was also something in his disappointment that went back to his time as an RAF chaplain. He had upset some of his friends in Intervarsity Christian Fellowship circles by taking a freer line on moderate use of alcohol in an officers' mess than was regarded as Christian. He had faced the issue of worldliness more thoroughly than I had up to then.

Subsequently I determined to think through my attitude to matters considered worldly. As a result of some shared thoughts I was asked to give a paper one year at the Southport Evangelical Conference. I called it 'The Pastor's Policy on Worldliness'. With some trepidation I presented it, expecting to be attacked as having undermined a true Christian approach. In fact the position I outlined was welcomed, and the paper later published in the quarterly, *The Churchman*. Today while deploring a great deal in the culture around us with its abandon of moral standards I am uninhibited in making use of what was once forbidden. Care should always be exercised by Christians in what I really believe is a decadent civilization. Although there is widespread welcome concern for justice and alleviation of world poverty the postmodern approach to life puts personal pleasure and gain above standards of moral restraint. In modern art, literature, drama nothing is barred. Proverbs tells us, 'where there is no vision, the people perish'. I favour the alternative translation, 'the people throw off restraints'.

Vision of God and his ways is lost for a majority in western civilization. As seeds of decay became evident in Roman civilization, so I suspect we are witnessing a similar decay. Liberals who follow the postmodern approach to life can be intolerant towards those advocating absolute standards.

## Moral questions

In former days evangelicals had a simple answer to moral questions. The Bible told us clearly what was right or wrong. Often the quoting of a single verse was all that was required. Why was alcohol forbidden to Christians? A verse such as, 'Be not drunk with wine wherein is excess' could be quoted. Other verses encouraging moderate use, or even that it can 'make glad the heart of man', were ignored. Anyway there was plenty of evidence in society to reveal abuse of alcohol. For other worldy pursuits, 'abstain from all appearance of evil' was sufficient guidance.

I soon came to see that isolated quotation was not the sure guide we need. For one thing, interpretation of Scripture across its range was essential. For another, there were moral problems in modern life for which the Bible had no direct word. And even where a direct word could be found, did it still apply? In the chapter on the Bible reference has been made to cultural change and temporary commands in Scripture applicable to the times given, but possibly not today. Should Christians support the death penalty? It is never abrogated in Scripture. Should Christians gain income from investments? Usury is not reinstated after being forbidden in the Mosaic Law.

Medical science has thrown up difficult moral questions not anticipated in Scripture. Artificial contraception greatly exercised non-Roman Christian bodies decades ago, and is still officially forbidden by Rome even if many adherents ignore the papal ruling. Abortion continues to divide Christians. I have come to the conclusion that in early stages of pregnancy, where life of the mother is threatened, or the embryo is seriously abnormal, or the result of rape of an under-age girl, abortion can be the lesser of two evils. Careful medical judgement is essential for these decisions. Thus I cannot go along with the absolute prohibition of pro-life groups. There are many moral problems not a choice between black and white, but between two greys.

Bound up with the abortion issue is the question when personhood begins. Some say it is at the moment of conception. Undoubtedly from that moment human life is present in the womb. The potential for personhood is present. But can two or four cells be called a person? Nature is profligate in the procreation of its species. Every plant and tree scatters many more seeds than can germinate and come to fruition. In the human species, like all other animate species, the female body produces more eggs than can ever produce living offspring. And more conceptions occur than can ever come to birth. Likewise male sperm are prolific in quantity. To be a person there needs to be the reality of relationship. For some time after conception the mother is not even conscious of the existence of the fertilized cells. Indeed a high proportion of these cells flush out of the body without the mother knowing. Later there can be a miscarriage. I don't believe these entities can be regarded as persons endowed with a spirit from God. What future can they have? The awkward question, if one accepts this line of thought, is: when is there a person, unique in value and part of God's created and saving order? Certainly at birth there is a person, but how soon before? I have to say, God alone knows. Possibly it is when development has sufficiently happened to allow a 'quickening'. Then the mother is related warmly to her child. Some psychologists and psychotherapists, such as the late Dr Frank Lake, believe the embryo after the development of the nervous system is experiencing its situation and storing memories that can cause personality problems in later life. I believe, therefore, that the time-limit for abortions needs to be reduced. This whole question is further complicated by the possibility of the embryo not coming to birth, and even being stillborn. While the Church must deal with great sympathy with the grieving parents, and provide a suitable service of committal, what is the place of that stillborn child in God's purpose? We cannot know.

I do not accept the contention that the mother has main responsibility in deciding for an abortion, on the grounds that it is her body. The embryo is not her body. In the case of severe abnormalities, more severe than, for instance, Down's syndrome, medical knowledge has to be carefully assessed. Personal convenience of parents ought not to be the deciding factor. Society has a responsibility for safeguarding embryos.

Another contentious moral problem over modern times has been divorce and remarriage. New Testament guidance is not as decisive as opponents of change would have the Church believe. The most direct word from Jesus on the matter occurs in a debate in which the aim of the Pharisees is to trap him into a lax or a rigid interpretation of the Law of Moses on divorce. As Bible commentators, including those of conservative stance, maintain, it is difficult to interpret Jesus' reply with its nuances as laying down a law for his followers in every age. Paul does not rule out a marriage after divorce.

In the Church of England over many decades the indissolubilist view prevailed, held by the Catholic tradition especially while it was dominant. A marriage properly entered into ought not to be dissolved, if we are obedient to God's will. Indissolubilists, however, maintained it was not possible for marriage to be dissolved. The maintenance of this line in the Roman Catholic tradition has led to what is a bizarre way of ending a marriage even when children have been born. The indissolubilist position has not always been followed by Anglo-Catholics. In the nineteenth century the saintly Bishop King of Lincoln had rejected it. However, with catholic dominance in the period between the wars in the twentieth century, and with growing alarm at the rising divorce rate, the Convocations of the Church of England passed regulations forbidding any marriage in church for a divorcee. The right of any priest under civil law to take such a marriage could not be removed, so the regulations only had moral force. Individual priests continued to exercise that right. In the latter part of the twentieth century efforts were made in the Church Assembly and then the General Synod to revoke the Convocation regulations. In spite of an increasing number of priests exercising their civil right the struggle was long and stirred deep emotions before coming to a successful conclusion. I was interested to find in my parish in Bolton the registers revealed a number of marriages of divorcees around wartime. The very Protestant vicar at the time probably thought that if Catholics would not allow it, he would.

I have long wanted the regulations to be rescinded. The basic issue was not the interpretation of particular biblical verses. It was the relationship of law and grace. Clearly the breakdown of a marriage with subsequent divorce was contrary to God's law. But in God's saving purposes the law does not have the last word. That is with grace. Unless grace triumphs, we are all as sinners lost. Divorce is not the sin that cannot be forgiven. Turning to God in penitence and faith every sinner is given a new start. Some marriages should not have happened. Not all marriages are made in heaven. Some churchfolk will go so far as to permit the Church to bless a new marriage but not allow such a blessing to be the full marriage service. This has seemed to me a miserly practice. The idea that those concerned should deny themselves as a contribution to the Church's witness to marriage seems a denial of pastoral concern and opportunity. The Church is asking persons who have gone through a bitter experience to bear alone the cost of the Church's witness. It is not the Church, nor the clergy, who bear the cost, but the couple, one of whom may be a church member. I have personal knowledge of persons after a divorce being refused a full marriage service in church suffering long-term spiritual damage. They were seeking God's help. In some cases the refusal was by an evangelical priest. What was he witnessing to by the refusal? Was it the gospel of God's loving-kindness and saving grace?

It is argued that vows made to one person and then abandoned cannot be made to another. While made in the presence of God and a congregation in a church marriage service, they are not made to God. We need to compare, and contrast them, with other vows. Baptismal vows, confirmation vows, ordination vows are made to God. Of those who made them who has never broken them? Yet by repentance and faith forgiveness is assured.

Some priests, perhaps a minority, adopt an all-comers' policy. Others believe some sensitive investigation is needed in case a church wedding would cause a scandal. If by some provision children of a former marriage are not being properly cared for, admittedly under difficult circumstances, if a new partner is perceived to have caused the earlier breakdown, a marriage in church could cause scandal. There may, of course, be individuals who resent such a marriage, especially if related to the former spouse, and this should be weighed in coming to a decision.

There was bound to be continuing divisions on how the decision should be taken. Was it left to the priest alone?

Should a bishop be involved? Would a panel to whom reference could or should be made be helpful? In 1983 after the General Synod had agreed on one of the options for moving to a replacement of the Convocation regulations a working group was appointed to make proposals. I was asked to chair it. The group had members who were indissolubilists in approach. The rest tried to accommodate their concerns, but we knew that in the end they would not support the report. A proposed handbook for use in the dioceses and parishes was prepared. When the report was presented to Synod the debate had to be adjourned before a vote. Between then and the next meeting of Synod bishops found considerable opposition among the clergy in the dioceses. It was no surprise, therefore, when Synod abandoned the project and turned the matter over to the bishops to come up with a solution, which after much delay they did. I was neither surprised, nor disappointed, that the work on the handbook had been in vain, even though one diocese asked me to let them have a copy. It could be too slanted to cater for the indissolubilist position. I was convinced that the way ahead is for the priest to make the decision, consulting with a bishop if he wishes when the situation is fraught with difficulties. In the community where I live a number of marriage requests after a divorce are coming in. Some are resulting in additions to the congregation.

Another emotion-riddled debate in General Synod was on cohabitation, increasingly evident even among church families. Speakers in the debate seemed to be expressing a widespread concern either because there were instances in their own families or at least feared there could be. There was the insistence that the Bible forbade sex outside marriage in a life-long union. I think we need to examine that assertion carefully. There is no ruling in Scripture that marriage can only be valid after a religious ceremony. In England before the Marriage Act of 1753 many couples just started living together. They might seek the Church's blessing in the service of holy matrimony but it was not compulsory. The concern of the State in the 1753 Act was to register all marriages for civil purposes, and the only way of registration was by the parish priest in the registers. The way marriage is regarded as being established depends on the culture concerned. New Testament evidence reveals a lengthy process of ceremonies with established customs within Jewish culture. And this testifies to the fact that society recognizes the marriage. It is not just a private arrangement between a couple. But it would appear from the Old Testament that a couple might enter into a sexual relationship, and when pregnancy followed, be married in the form of their culture.

The basic question in cohabitation is, do the couple intend it to be permanent, a life-long relationship? Or, is it regarded as an arrangement as long as they want it? For this reason the Church must advocate the wisdom of entering into a marriage, so that God's pattern for humanity is followed, that children may find security, and that society can acknowledge the union. But a judgemental attitude towards those cohabiting, when, for instance, they bring a child for baptism, is to be avoided. Sensitive encouragement is the way to deal with this pastoral opportunity. A high proportion of those seeking a wedding in church are already cohabiting. They should be warmly welcomed.

The most contentious moral issue at present surrounds homosexuality, threatening to disrupt communion between Anglicans. Although much talk about communion is confused, the threat to relationships is real. There is little realistic debate, much sniping at a distance from entrenched positions. As in trench warfare in World War One it is difficult to see how progress can be made when each side demands capitulation. All contentious issues between Christians demand honest, charitable discussion in pursuit of truth.

Much attention has been focused on the Lambeth 1998 resolution on the subject. I was present at the plenary session where that resolution was accepted by a large majority. Beforehand a section of the conference drawing together a wide representation of views had spent ten days of unhurried debate, arriving at an agreed statement. This seemed to be ignored by the hundreds of bishops in the plenary session. It could hardly be said that there was a debate; rather the rehearsal of preconceived positions with much emotion. However, the last clause of the resolution clearly acknowledged that the debate was not finalized. The primates and the ACC were asked to go on monitoring the debate, something which has not yet really happened.

I make my own position clear. I am unambiguously heterosexual. I have a deep emotional aversion to homosexual practices, certainly between men. This goes back 60 years to my time in the Navy. I am bound to approach the issue from an evangelical, traditionalist position, but less than happy with the way that has been generally presented over the last few years.

I am convinced there are persons who are genetically, unalterably homosexual in orientation. Not all who claim to be gay or lesbian fall into that category. By accident of early nurture some may come to homosexual orientation. And others in the period of adolescence, while confused about their sexuality, may be persuaded into the orientation. Some gays and lesbians are guilty of seeking recruits to their cause. Whatever rights they certainly have, and however justified in combating discrimination, it is not right to target vulnerable young people especially in a society that encourages all manner of sexual expression and experiment as a matter of rights.

Opponents in the debate quote authorities supporting their own position on the question of genetic, unalterable orientation. After all, if infants can be born with incurable diseases the same may be true of sexual orientation. Nature does not produce perfect, normal individuals all the time.

A study of reviews of the biblical evidence leaves me still less than absolutely convinced we are rightly interpreting and rightly applying the texts. Serious questions remain in my mind. The concerns about biblical interpretation mentioned earlier are relevant here. Is Paul in Romans 1 referring to a permanent relationship between Christians of the same sex? Or is promiscuous homosexual activity and pederasty, both prevalent in the culture then, what Paul has in mind? The activities he condemns are, he says, the consequence of pagan attitudes of those who have not acknowledged the true God. God has 'given them over' to disgusting practices. What about Christians who are homosexual?

Attempt has been made to solve the issue by referring to marriage and nature. No Christian can doubt that God's will for humanity is marriage for life with consequent care of children. But for those of unalterable homosexual orientation to be pushed however gently into marriage is a recipe for disaster. There are cases of persons entering into marriage, becoming parents and subsequently recognizing they are homosexual. The phenomena of trans-sexual change relates here. We need to address the fact that on the scale of human sexuality not everyone is clearly at one end or the other. Some are at varying degrees in between. Appeal to nature is inconclusive. There are species in which homosexual activity is known alongside regular sexual activity.

The whole argument is bedevilled in my judgement by the failure, out of delicacy, to identify what is meant by homosexual practices. Condemnation of practices without indicating what is in mind is irresponsible. Is everyone assuming it is sodomy? Undoubtedly for men it can be. But what about women? There are other expressions of intimacy and mutual erotic satisfaction besides sodomy, followed by married heterosexuals as well as homosexuals on occasions. Mutual masturbation and other physical contacts have to be considered. Between two persons who love each other intimate contact seems an obvious expression. Whatever else we are, we are all psychosomatic beings. The question, therefore, to face is, if two Christians of homosexual orientation live together do we leave them to decide before God what is appropriate and right? I have known in my parishes two men, one a godly evangelical retired priest of homosexual orientation, the other a sidesman, living in the same small house, and two women, loyal members of the congregation living likewise. Was it any part of my responsibility as a pastor to ask what they got up to in their homes? The retired priest was a remarkable man who was much help to me and my wife. He had led to faith in Christ the boy who became Dr Frank Lake, no doubt because of the way he was he had a warm interest in boys and young men. He told Frank he had to be a medical missionary and he would find funds for his training as a doctor. Frank came to preach at the old man's funeral which I took. Years before Frank had confirmed that his benefactor was certainly of homosexual orientation but was not, he believed, involved in homosexual activities. It seemed to me that God used that man's nature to be a blessing to more than just Frank. But today a priest and another man living in a very close relationship would be regarded with harsh criticism by some Christians. What outcry would follow if a priest speaking of a male friend echoed the words of David about Jonathan, 'your love to me was wonderful, surpassing the love of women'.

I do, however, recognize that in today's climate if clergy are living with someone of the same sex they should be told by their bishop that if a scandal is caused in their parish and area, and it cannot be satisfactorily answered, drastic action could follow. It is for this reason that I believe a tougher line should apply to clergy than to laity. I have no sympathy or support for the American Church in appointment as bishop of a homosexual divorced from his wife and publicly living with a male partner and apparently not celibate. In that case there was indeed substantial scandal, apart from its damaging effect in the Anglican Communion.

I have no doubt my statements will not find agreement with many evangelicals. I do not want to be insensitive. My aim has been to raise questions that need to be faced and answered convincingly if we are to present a convincing statement of the truth. In answering them all signs of homophobia must be avoided. In the long run the way the Church deals with this difficult issue will have an effect on the rest of society. We can make it easier or harder to evangelize. Fierce crossness cannot ease the gospel's appeal. The media will not be a helpful ally. I sometimes question the fierceness of some evangelical pronouncements in this matter. A hymn by F. W. Faber, a nineteenth-century Catholic, comes to mind. Its use was discouraged in evangelical circles in the past because he was a Catholic. One verse says, 'For the love of God is broader than the measures of man's mind.' The next verse now omitted in some books goes, 'But we make his love too narrow by false limits of our own, and we magnify his strictness with a zeal he will not own.'

It is certain that registration of the status of homosexual couples who intend it to last will be taken up in this country by many, not least by Christians. What all Christians must do, in my opinion, is to resist all attempts to use the term 'marriage' and related measures that undermine the unique nature of marriage.

One last word. I wonder why Christians get into such a fervour on matters of sex, and seem to put sexual sins at the top of the list of what God condemns. Of course, sex touches us all at the deepest level. But in passages in the Epistles where sexual sins are mentioned, other expressions of sinful human nature do not get as much attention.

There is absolutely no doubt that sexual immorality is condemned, but specific instances of such sin are seldom mentioned. Most of the Bible's condemnation of sexual sins are about adultery, the taking of another's wife or husband. Even this can be forgiven, as Jesus showed and David found, when there is penitence.

In my earlier years in the evangelical tradition, sex seemed to be surrounded with shame, even guilt. While decent regard for this most intimate of relationships is appropriate, the element of taboo was strong. And in an age where attitudes towards sex have gone to the other extreme, and moral restraints abandoned, it is understandable if Christians express concern and revulsion. But throughout Christian history from the Fathers, through the collapse of the Roman civilization accompanied by sexual licentiousness, in the centuries of the Western Church ruled by males and the more modern debates involving contraception, a positive and joyful attitude to sex has not been very evident. This seems to be in contrast with the best expressions of Hebrew thought as evident in the Song of Solomon. Are Christians embarrassed to have that book in the Bible? They tend to spiritualize its message. It may be argued that our marriage services express a positive and glad acceptance of this God-given most natural aspect of human life and relationships, and clergy in marriage preparation can present that positive approach. But all too readily the media and public commentators seize opportunities from church reactions to subject the faith to ridicule. It is going to get harder to present a positive Christian witness, but the times demand it.

# Still Evangelical?

The title of this book is *Evangelical and Evolving*. The second adjective is not in doubt, is the first still appropriate? In 2003 my wife and I on a brief visit to Italy were in Rome at a weekend. Our hotel was near the Basilica of St Paul without the Walls. On the Sunday morning we sat at the back of the congregation while Mass was conducted in Italian. At the peace we were warmly greeted by those near us. Knowing the structure of the service I tried to turn the occasion into my own act of worship. During the sermon the thought crossed my mind, these folk know they are Roman Catholics in obedience to the Pope – how do I describe myself? The answer I came up with then was, a Reformed Catholic Evangelical. Certainly I have a deeper appreciation of the Catholic tradition of the Church then when I began in the ministry. I have learned and been helped by that tradition but have seen the need for constant reformation. I have been helped in search for the truth by insights of the liberal tradition. That tradition has led me to go on asking questions of what I believe. Questioning my evangelical tradition has convinced me that finding more and more of the truth – indeed to question and test severely what I believe – is of greater importance than simply maintaining a tradition. On occasions, though not frequently, I must ask myself whether in my commitment to the Christian faith over 80 years I might possibly be self-deluded. After all, I see around me in the world many people who seem possessed by strong delusions. An obvious example is the extreme fundamentalist Muslim suicide bomber, believing his action will lead straight to Paradise where a group of maidens will surround him. He is sure God has revealed his will. My testing of the reality of my faith in Christ has led to stronger conviction. Doubting is not unbelieving, it can result in greater faith. I have known Christians who in their approach of death seem to have lost their faith, with consequent confusion of those who knew them. It could in some cases be a result of illness affecting their minds. But as I linger in heaven's waiting-room I want to be ever clearer of my trust in Christ.

At the heart of my conviction as an evangelical is faith in Jesus Christ crucified and risen. From childhood I knew that Jesus died for our sins. Sometimes the atonement was presented in rather crude terms – God punished Jesus instead of us. What I learned from P. T. Forsyth and James Denney was a fuller, richer, more wonderful understanding of the atonement. Forsyth was very strong in his emphasis on the holiness of God as well as the love of God. Forsyth speaks of God

> as self-complete and absolute moral personality, the universal and eternal holy God whose sufficency is of Himself, the self-contained, and self-determined moral reality of the universe, for which all things work together in a supreme concursus, which must endure if all else fails, and must be secured at any loss beside.[23]

He saw the moral order as ultimately more significant than the physical order discoverable by scientific exploration. The physical order is of time, the moral eternal. Holiness must judge sin and separate the sinner from the divine presence. God loves the sinner. The only solution to the divine dilemma was for God himself to suffer the judgement of sin in himself and by that suffering self-sacrifice win the sinner to repentance and faith. Thus reconciliation and redemption are achieved. The cross was in the heart of God from eternity. Knowing that his human creature, given the will to obey or to turn against him, would sin, along with creation would come salvation. Jesus was 'the Lamb slain before the foundation of the world'. In Forsyth's own words. 'God's holiness issues to man in love, acts upon sin in grace, and exercises grace through judgement.' So, the cross is from first to last an act of God, the Holy Trinity, its sacrifice is rendered within humanity by the Son, but by 'no third party'. It is by God himself in his Son. The central action of the atonement at the cross is glimpsed in the cry of derelictione, where separation, in a way mortals can only dimly perceive, is borne within the Trinity. The atonement is beyond doubt a trinitarian event. Jürgen Moltmann in *The Crucified God* has further helped my understanding.[24] He dares to speak of God against God in that Cry of Dereliction. Because Jesus, the Son of God, suffered that hell of separation, the sinner need not suffer it.

It has become increasingly common in recent times to speak of the vulnerability of God. This is usually in response to the challenge to theodicy posed by the injustice and innocent suffering in the world caused by human evil and natural disasters. If God is omnipotent and loving, why does he not intervene to stop it happening? is a question that seems to have no answer. Christians used to try to answer by emphasizing the sovereignty of God. He works out his sovereign will; we will never know in this life why he allows such suffering, but one day in heaven we will. A collect in the Book of Common Prayer begins 'O God who ordereth all things in Heaven and Earth'. I can no longer use that prayer. I do not believe the massacre of innocent victims by a fanatical suicide bomber is God's will, nor the murder of a child by a sex pervert, nor fatal cancer in a young mother. Our thinking needs to start with the nature of true love. And love in God is essentially his will acting for the blessing of the loved one. Love is vulnerable to the response of the loved one. The God who is love in creating the universe and all within it, including ourselves, made himself vulnerable to his creature, allowing what was created the freedom to be and develop. This was the basis of evolution. His love is as operative in creation as in redemption. It is not by absolute control, compulsion, that everything came to be. This is not to imagine God as a helpless observer. The loved one can be influenced by love, by approaches that woo, with the intention to benefit and work for the other's well-being. Science recognizes a certain openness to new developments in evolution.

As the human species evolved from other earlier species God may be thought of as guiding humans not only to self-consciousness but to a sense of the numinous, to belief that there was more than the world of time and space. Hence the concept of the spirit-world and an after-life emerged. We may say in his love God took the risk of humanity developing false religious ideas. And in time God brought his human creature to God-consciousness, perhaps with a single individual or couple, the Adam and Eve of Genesis. The early chapters of Genesis may be taken as expressing this development in pictorial, non-scientific story form. But then, as Genesis 3 teaches, to be God-conscious did not inevitably lead to loving, obedient response to God's love. He was vulnerable to human sin. And so the love active in creation began the path to redemption of the sinful loved one. That path was all of God's initiative and self-chosen action at total cost to himself. The end was to be atonement and the bringing of his beloved creature to a final goal in glory.

I hesitate to use adjectives before the noun atonement – penal, substitutionary, etc. – not because they don't express some truth, but because the wonder of the cross is multi-faceted. It is the victory over all the forces of hell. Christ's victory was won on Calvary. It was not a case of Easter Day reversing a defeat on Good Friday – Christus Victor is the Christ of the cross. He reigns from the tree. The cross is also the way God deals with all the evil, injustice, innocent suffering of the world. It is where theodicy is demonstrated and realized. Moltmann, facing up to all the injustice, cruelty and inexplicable evil, particularly in the modern world, answers the questions – Where is God in all this? Is he a God of love and power? Why then does he not act? He begins the answer by posing the further question, What sort of a God is one who allows his Son to suffer unjustly the hatred and cruelty of humanity? He is a God who takes it all into himself, suffers with, alongside those who suffer and sustains them by his love and grace, knowing that the outcome is resurrection. Not merely empathy in suffering, but a glorious hope is offered. This is grace in action. Grace expresses all I have known of God's dealings with those who, won by his love, turn to him. 'Oh to Grace, how great a debtor daily I'm constrained to be!'

R. W. Dale, a famous preacher of the nineteenth century, could ask while Forsyth was still in his forties, 'Who is this P. T. Forsyth? He has recovered for us a word we had all but lost – the word Grace.' If anyone claims to be dependent entirely on the grace of God through Jesus Christ crucified and risen, that one is a brother or sister in God's family whatever differences of understanding of aspects of truth we may have. This has to be the basis for all controversies affecting the Church at all times.

The resurrection was indeed a bodily resurrection. No corpse was left behind, but the crucified body was transformed; no longer subject to decay, pain, death. It was the foretaste and guarantee of the resurrection body that redeemed spirits will inherit at Christ's parousia. What can the believing Christian expect from the time of death till that parousia? A reverent agnosticism is called for. The nature of eternity and its relationship to time is beyond our grasp. Inevitably, emotion and sentiment come into play. The fate of the present body we know, cremated to ashes or gradual break-up in the ground or in the sea. What happens to the soul, the spirit? Bereaved persons like to think of the departed joining others gone before. Mother is now with father. Some even think the departed loved one is still near at hand, watching over them. My own conviction is that these thoughts owe more to sentiment than reality. I do not believe the departed are able to be aware of the life and situations of those left behind. As Christian we can say that they are at rest and in peace. May they rest in peace, is our usual prayer. How could they be at peace if they are aware of all we who are left are going through, our pains, worries, failures, sins? Nor do I believe there can be any communication with them, whatever mediums claim. Indeed for these reasons I cannot pray to the saints. Indeed I see no reason to, when I can come to God's throne of grace through the one mediator, Christ Jesus, aided by the Holy Spirit, who knows the mind of God as well as knowing me better than I know myself. I have no problem with prayers in respect of the departed in Christ. At every Eucharist, and frequently at other times, I thank God for all I received from him through loved ones now with him, for their present rest in him, and for the glorious hope of resurrection and reunion at the parousia. Evangelicals used to get very worked up at the concept of prayers for the dead. This stems from opposition to the concept that the status and fate of the departed could be changed by prayer of those left behind. Prayers in respect of the departed, however, can be expressions of our faith and hope in God, as clearly as the prayer, 'Thy will be done'. The statement of belief in the creed in the communion of saints is a recognition that the Church living and the Church departed are one still in the Body of Christ.

There is another aspect of prayers and the departed I believe in. Although they are not aware of my life now on earth, I believe the prayers they offered for me while they were alive are still being answered by God. The prayers did not become ineffective with their death. And the prayers I have offered for my children and grandchildren, for instance, since they were born will go on being answered after I am gone. What, then is the state of the departed in what, for want of a better understanding, we call the intermediate state? The New Testament gives us a few glimpses. Believers are 'with Christ', they are 'asleep', but that may refer particularly to the bodily existence. Martyrs are said to be 'waiting', pleading 'How long, O Lord, how long?' It seems unthinkable that one who has known the peace and joy of the Lord while on earth is deprived of that in his immediate presence.

All, however long they may have been on the Christian way, arrive at death still far from perfection in holiness. But the New Testament promises transformation into the likeness of Christ. St Paul anticipating the change speaks of it as 'in the twinkling of an eye', but in the context of the same chapter he seems to be referring to the bestowal of the resurrection body. In the first epistle of John there is the admission that we do not know what we shall become, but there is confidence that 'we shall be like him for we shall see him as he is'. Transformation by beholding is a theme elsewhere in Scripture, even as far back as Moses on Mount Sinai. This work of transformation is to be going on while in this life but can never be final here. Charles Wesley sums it up in the words of a hymn: 'changed from glory into glory, 'till in heaven we take our place'.

STILL EVANGELICAL?

Are we to expect a sudden and complete transformation at Christ's parousia? The Reformers rejected the idea of purgatory, a place of spiritual improvement for which masses for the dead could be offered. They emphasized the complete acceptance of those justified by grace through faith alone, and so there was no doubt about the saved status of such. But justification is not the same as complete sanctification. We must recognize that all who enter heaven are not saintly, elderly believers. There are children whose lives are tragically cut short, mentally disabled persons who in a simple way trust God, and many lives lost in wars and natural disasters. What does transformation mean for them? In the end we must leave our unanswered questions with God.

What we can say with assurance is that to be baptized into the death and resurrection of God is to be received into the very life of the Trinity. That is while on this earth. St Paul can say to Christian readers 'Your life is hid with Christ in God'. It can be nothing less than that for the departed soul. And with no sin to cloud or harm that relationship the transformation is certain, if the how or when is not yet known to us. The hiddenness Paul speaks of suggests absolute security.

I do not envisage heaven as a place of peaceful inactivity. It would be consistent with God's dealings with us in this life for us to find exploration, discovery, an entering into the riches of the divine nature. Shall we ever come to an end of discovering the riches of God's life? Fully to comprehend him would suggest equality with God. The discovery, however, will be in the corporate relationship with the whole company of the redeemed. That is how it is to be on earth, so it will be in heaven.

In creation, as science reveals, there is a certain openness for hitherto unknown developments. Within the freedom of God to bring about new things, he has afforded freedom of human persons to bring about new things. Intercessory prayer has its validity in this provision. Through believing and obedient prayer God works with us to bring about what otherwise would not be. It is possible that, in the consummation of God's new creation, an openness for new things to God's glory may be shared by us.

After the death of the body, what goes on to eternity with God? The words 'soul' and 'spirit' are used. Are the two synonymous? Scripture uses both but some references seem to indicate a difference in understanding. 'Soul' seems to stand for the life principle in a person, and that person's personality; the essential 'me' known to others more or less according to relationship, but known in a different degree to the self. It is an amalgam of the history of experiences, memories, interplay of genes and environment, influence of relationships, faults, failings, achievements and emotions. Dr John Polkinghorne, priest and physicist, has written of the soul as developmental. In old age what makes anyone the same person as in childhood is not any material continuity. The DNA remains the same, but the atoms are being renewed all the time. There is, however, a developing pattern of personality through the complex influence of many factors. So, he maintains, the soul is not something given at a single instant of existence. Some Christians regard the soul as given by God at the moment of conception. The developmental concept runs contrary to this. In the first days after conception the few cells have the potential for personhood. It is one of the essential qualities of personhood to be in relationship. But at that stage even the mother will not know of their existence. And, as previously noted, many such cells are lost naturally. It seems impossible to regard those thwarted forms of life as persons.

If the soul is developmental, what is the spirit? Scripture refers to the spirit as given by God. 'The spirit returns to God who gave it.' Is it an entity given to all, and if so, how and when? If given at conception, what is the purpose if the embryo at an early stage is to be lost, as many are? Can we say that the spirit is the capacity to relate to God, the Eternal Spirit? The spiritual truth of the early chapters of Genesis is that God bestows that capacity. But as a result of sin, failure to respond with trust and obedience, not only is that God-given capacity unfulfilled, but separation from God – spiritual death – ensues.

The theme of the gospel, however, is that God will not give up on humanity. He aims to restore, giving his life to replace spiritual death. 'The wages of sin is death [not physical but spiritual], but the gift of God is eternal life.' Relationship is established by God's life in the soul of the human person who will receive it. The spirit is redeemed. Receiving God's reconciling love restores the capacity to relate to him. And thenceforth the soul thus possessing eternal life is to seek to grow spiritually into the likeness of Christ. It is in accord with these understandings that I am inclined to the concept of conditional immortality, spiritual life for ever being conditional upon receiving God's gift in grace. This concept is in contrast with that of eternal spirits for ever damned in separation from God, although I recognize references in Scripture that can seem to support it.

Attitude to the Bible is generally held by evangelicals to be a major test of their orthodoxy. I have already indicated belief that the Bible brings to us the wholly trustworthy God-given presentation of the way of salvation and will of God for us. The Scriptures are our final authority for faith and conduct, the sacrament of the word of God, which coming to us in convicting and redeeming power brings us to submit to Christ as Lord and Saviour. It is, however, essential that we interpret the Scriptures and apply them aright. Anyone can be guilty of reading into the Bible what they want or expect to find. It has gone on throughout church

history. The Bible is not a scrapbook of theological statements to be selected to suit our preconceptions. The Holy
Spirit is given to understand the Scriptures aright, I am
happy, however, with the Anglican emphasis on the role of
tradition and reason within the contemporary experience of
the Church in the task of interpretation. Tradition, reason,
experience are not by their nature infallible guides but they
are needed for the prevention of errors of private interpretation. To sum up, I am totally committed to Article 6 of the
Articles of Religion. Is that not sufficient for evangelicals?

It is the fact of Christ, his incarnation, death and resurrection, that convinces me of the truth of the Christian faith.
Whatever the relationship of God to other religions and their
adherents I cannot really know, although I believe that if any
human being is finally to enjoy God's acceptance it will be on
the basis of the redeeming work effected by God in his
sacrifice on the cross. That self-giving in love to deal with
human sin I see to be essential to the salvation of anyone. Its
saving effect, though enacted once in history extends over all
time, before and since. The believing Hebrew who could
never do more than anticipate from hints that his God had a
saving purpose to be fulfilled is covered by the atonement.
Concerning any other individual who had never heard of
Christ or not understood his saving significance, I can only
adhere to the ancient confession: 'Shall not the judge of all
the earth do right?'

The convincing and converting facts about Jesus Christ are
these. All he said or was said about him adds up to the conclusion he was the incarnate Son of God, or else mad or bad,
as C. S. Lewis emphasized. Then, the atonement accom-
plished by the Trinity at Calvary convincingly deals with the
fundamental problem for humanity, sin and estrangement
from God, and the universal problem of evil. Only by God's
action can primacy of morality in the universe be ensured.

Further, the resurrection of Christ, inaugurating and establishing the new creation, is the only ground for hope. Without that hope there is only the collapse of the universe to look forward to. 'If only in this life we have hope, we are of all men to be pitied.' And, finally, God in Christ through his Holy Spirit has changed, and is going on changing me.

It is the faith outlined above that I have sought to proclaim over the years. Its presentation has changed, developed as grasp of truth has enlarged. A former vicar friend to whom I owed much, William Leatham, at Keele 1967, said: 'Much preaching is too small to be believed, and too easy to be effective . . . And too confident to be true.' He further maintained: 'A closed mind is a denial of the Holy Spirit . . . and evangelicals in the twentieth century have not been conspicuous for their open-mindedness.'

Just before the Keele Congress at the Islington Clerical Conference its chairman, Peter Johnston said:

> The Church of England is changing. Indeed, it is in a state of ferment – although it remains to be seen whether fermentation will result in a mature vintage. On the other hand, Evangelicals in the Church of England are changing too. Not in doctrinal conviction (for the truth of the Gospel cannot change), but (like any healthy child) in stature and in posture. It is a tragic thing, however, that Evangelicals have a very poor image in the Church as a whole. We have acquired a reputation for narrow partisanship and obstructionism . . . We need to repent and change . . . We who love the adjective evangelical, because it declares us to be gospel-men [sic], must take great care, therefore, that what we are seeking to defend and champion is the Gospel in all its biblical fullness and not some party shibboleth or tradition of doubtful biblical pedigree.

Evangelicals at the beginning of the twenty-first century have moved forward since Keele 1967. They are stronger in numbers than for perhaps a century, have a broad spectrum, and are more influential in the structures of the Church and in theological colleges. But in recent years they have been more divided, not about the person and work of Christ, salvation, grace, the Trinity, the gospel, but about interpretation of Scripture and how to relate to other traditions in the Church. Underlying the division may be detected a difference in basic attitudes – have we got it all right, a full grasp of the truth, or could our understanding need any correction or development as we debate with others? To reduce this issue to a matter of submission to the authority of the Bible is too simplistic.

What is it we are defending when we fiercely oppose interpretation of Scripture promoted by others? Is it really the honour of God? Or our own firm convictions that we have got it right? Do we feel deep down that if we admit that possibly there may be revisions of understanding to be accepted, our inner security is threatened? To repeat a point made earlier, our inner security is only ultimately and completely in our relationship with our Creator Lord and Saviour.

I have previously expressed my debt to the first volume by Mark A. Noll in the five-volume *A History of Evangelicalism* in which he deals with the years from 1740 onwards. I quote from his final summary of that first period:

At its worst, the new evangelicalism neglected, caricatured and distorted inherited traditions of Reformation Protestantism. Evangelical beliefs and practices could foster a self-centred, egoistic and narcissistic spirituality and also create new arenas for destructive spiritual competition. From in-group clichés, associations and institutions, evangelicals sometimes constructed new barriers to alienate humans from each other. They could turn so obsessively inward to ignore the structures of social evil. Most important, evangelicals could trivialize the Christian Gospel by treating it as a ballyhooed commodity to be hawked for its power to soothe a nervous, dislocated people in the opening cultural markets of the expanding British empire.

But at its best evangelicalism provided needed revitalization to English-speaking Protestant Christianity. It breathed vibrant religious life into stagnant or confused religious institutions. It created dynamic communities of self-giving love and international networks of supporting fellowship. It reached out to many at the margins of respectable society. From authentic personal experience it provided a dynamism for addressing corporate evils. Most important, it communicated the beauty and the power of the Christian Gospel in a wide variety of settings and through that Gospel provided a wide range of individuals with purpose before God and meaning for this life, and it did so for the long haul.

Evangelicalism was never static, nor simply given. Right from the start, the energy that brought the movement into existence pushed on to further innovations, expanded the depths and breadth of its reach, suffered from countless missteps, divided into hotly competing fragments and entered into ever-new connections with the broader society. Always at the centre was engagement with the Gospel.[25]

I believe that assessment of the beginnings of our evangelical tradition, based on a full, thoroughly researched study of those early days, can well serve to assess our position and performance today.

In the Introduction I indicated that this is a personal story. It is not a statement of what all who call themselves open evangelicals believe. A tradition, while remaining committed to its basic foundation truths, must evolve if it is to remain alive and responsive to new truth. Understanding the truth of God in Christ is a journey, not a destination arrived at some time in the past. Throughout our earthly pilgrimage of discipleship we are to be open to whatever new truths God has for us. I really believe that in heaven we will enter more and more fully into the mystery of God's person. That makes it an exciting prospect. In the meantime if anything in this book helps others to check up on their beliefs it will have served its purpose.

# References

1 Graham Kings, 'Canal, River and Rapids: Contemporary Evangelicalism in the Church of England', *Anvil*, Vol. 20, No. 3, p. 171.

2 Mark A. Noll, *The Rise of Evangelicalism: The Age of Edwards, Whitefield, and the Wesleys (History of Evangelicalism, Vol. 1)*, Leicester, IVP, 2003.

3 Mark A. Noll, *The Scandal of the Evangelical Mind*, Leicester, IVP, 1994, p. 133.

4 P. T. Forsyth, *The Principle of Authority*, London, Independent Press, 2nd edn 1952, pp. 2, 3.

5 James Orr, *Revelation and Inspiration*, New York, Scribners, 1910, pp. 197, 198.

6 Quoted by A. B. Bruce in *Inspiration and Inerrancy* (1891), p. 4. Quotations in 3 and 4 are taken up by James D. G. Dunn in *The Living Word*, London, SCM Press, 1987 – a most thorough and convincing critique of the inerrancy school in the evangelical tradition from Warfield and Hodge onwards.

7 John Webster, *Holy Scripture – a Dogmatic Sketch*, Cambridge, Cambridge University Press, 2003, pp. 13, 31.

8 Richard Briggs, *Reading the Bible Wisely*, London, SPCK, 2003, p. 17.

9 Howard Marshall (ed.), *New Testament Introduction*, Carlisle, Paternoster Press, 1977, p. 132.

10 James Denny, *Studies in Theology*, 1885, p. 1.

11 Kenneth A. Locke, *Anvil*, Vol. 14, No. 3, 1997, p. 24.

12 Noll, *The Scandal of the Evangelical Mind*, pp. 50-1.

13 John Howe with Colin Craston, *Anglicanism and the Universal Church*, Toronto, Anglican Book Centre, 1990, p. 31.

14 Howe and Craston, *Anglicanism and the Universal Church*, p. 30.

15 Stephen W. Sykes, *Authority in the Anglican Communion: Essays Presented to Bishop John Howe*, Toronto, Anglican Book Centre, 1987, p. 284.

16 *Bonds of Affection: Proceedings of ACC-6, Badagry, Nigeria 1984*, London, Church House, 1985, p. 60ff.

17 *Mission in a Broken World: Report of ACC-8, Wales 1990*, London, Church House, p. 100.

18 Howe and Craston, *Anglicanism and the Universal Church*, p. 17.

19 Colin Craston (ed.), *Open to the Spirit: Anglicans and the Experience of Renewal*, London, Church House, 1987.

20 Colin O. Buchanan, *Growing Into Union. The Clarified Scheme Examined: An Analysis of Anglican–Methodist Unity*, Bramcote, Grove Books, 1971, p. 74ff.

21 Buchanan, *Growing Into Union*, p. 71.

22 Jürgen Moltmann, *Theology of Hope*, London, SCM Press, 1967.

23 P. T. Forsyth, *Preaching and the Modern Mind*, USA, R. A. Kessinger, 2003, p. 241.

24 Jürgen Moltmann, *The Crucified God*, London, SCM Press, 1974.

25 Noll, *Rise of Evangelicalism*, pp. 292, 293.

# Index